GOLD BEACH - JIG
JIG Sector and West

With the continued expansion of the Battleground series a **Battleground Series Club** has been formed to benefit the reader. The purpose of the Club is to keep members informed of new titles and to offer many other reader-benefits. Membership is free and by registering an interest you can help us predict print runs and thus assist us in maintaining the quality and prices at their present levels.

Please call the office 01226 734555, or send your name and address along with a request for more information to:
Battleground Series Club Pen & Sword Books Ltd,
47 Church Street, Barnsley, South Yorkshire S70 2AS

Photograph previous page: Bren gun carriers of the 1st Dorsetshire Regiment, with deep wading kit fitted, come ashore on the afternoon of D-Day.

Battleground Europe
NORMANDY

GOLD BEACH - JIG
JIG Sector and West

Tim Saunders

LEO COOPER

Dedicated to my uncle,
Major George Boultwood, The Devonshire Regiment,
attached to the Combined Operations Staff,
who was severely wounded en route to
Port en Bessin

Other books in the series by Tim Saunders
Hill 112 – Normandy
Hell's Highway – Market Garden
Nijmegen – Market Garden
The Island – Market Garden

Published by
LEO COOPER
an imprint of
Pen & Sword Books Limited
47 Church Street, Barnsley, South Yorkshire S70 2AS
Copyright © Tim Saunders, 2002

ISBN 0 85052 866 6

A CIP catalogue of this book is available
from the British Library

Printed by CPI UK

For up-to-date information on other titles produced under the Leo Cooper
imprint, please telephone or write to:
Pen & Sword Books Ltd, FREEPOST, 47 Church Street
Barnsley, South Yorkshire S70 2AS
Telephone 01226 734222

CONTENTS

ACKNOWLEDGEMENTS

In writing this book, I have relied on the peerless and comprehensive accounts given by all the major units of 231 Infantry Brigade and others. These 'others' include my late and much loved uncle, Major George Boultwood (Devonshire Regiment), who was author of the Combined Operations pamphlet, issued in preparation for the invasion of Japan. Directed by Lord Mountbatten, he used the landing by 231 Brigade on JIG Beach as an example of how an amphibious operation should be conducted. Together with official documentation, members of 231 Brigade Group have left the most comprehensive account of all the British D-Day landings. I am proud to be able to present their words through the *Battleground Europe Series* to a wider audience than many of them probably ever expected.

I am particularly grateful to my own Regimental Museum's staff in Dorchester and to Colonel Daroch of the Royal Hampshires Museum at Winchester for their help. I would also like to acknowledge the patience of my family for sitting or playing on various parts of JIG Beach, while I went 'concrete hunting' along and behind the beach. Thank you for tolerating my military history activities while we were supposedly on holiday.

INTRODUCTION

In October 1940, Winston Churchill concluded a broadcast to the French people:

> *'Goodnight then. Sleep, to gather strength for the morning. For the morning will come: brightly will it shine on the brave and true: kindly on all who suffer for the cause. Vive la France! Alors bon nuit. Domez bien...'*

My first visit to JIG Sector of GOLD Beach was on a cycle trip with my brother in 1976, while I was on leave from Sandhurst. Some years later, during a tour of the Normandy battlefields, with the then Major Paul Newton of the Royal Hampshires, our group of trainees was being conducted along the invasion coast by a 'guide' from a tour company. The guide's comment as we passed through Courseules-sur-Mer was: 'This is JUNO Beach where the Canadians landed'. The young soldiers were far too polite to point out that they had already guessed this from the profusion of maple leaf flags around the town. However, when we reached GOLD Beach and le Hamel, where our regiments landed, Paul Newton's patience was at an end. 'Tim, you've got a book on this, get them off the coach and tell'em what happened!' Well used to the Army's habit of casting individuals as 'experts', I stepped off the coach, clutching my tatty copy of Brigadier 'Speedy' Bredin's book *Three Assault Landings*. I survived this encounter with a highly critical audience – just; and I have been back to JIG many times since – better prepared!

Over the years, it has become obvious to me that the landing of 231 Brigade was the most difficult of all the British D-Day landings. Not only were the beaches and ground behind JIG unfavourable, but the West Countrymen were also facing Germans of the same field grade division that nearly caused the abandonment of the American assault on OMAHA.

In recognition of the difficulties, the experienced 231 Brigade, together with 47 Commando Royal Marines, were allocated the crucial JIG Beach, having already landed in both Sicily and Italy. Not only were they required to breach the German Atlantic Wall and take objectives three miles inland but also to exploit ten miles west and link up with the Americans, who were to strike east from OMAHA Beach.

This book tells the story of how 231 Brigade Group became one of the few formations to all but complete its D-Day objectives in the time allocated, despite having to overcome difficulties that were both expected and unexpected.

Advice to Visitors

Preparation and planning are important prerequisites for an enjoyable and successful tour. This section aims to give some advice to those who are travelling to Normandy for the first time and acts as a checklist for the regular visitor.

Travel to Normandy

Most visitors travelling to the Normandy battlefields do so by car. However, with the area's proximity to ports, an increasing number of hardy souls are cycling around the battlefields. However one chooses to travel around Normandy, a journey originating in the UK has to cross the Channel. A wide range of options is available. The nearest ferry service to Arromanches is the Brittany Ferries route which delivers the visitor from Portsmouth to Ouistreham, less than an hour's drive from JIG Beach. This crossing is slightly longer than others, being six hours during the day or six hours thirty minutes overnight. Further away, over an hour to the west, is the port of Cherbourg, which is served by sailings from Portsmouth, Southampton and Poole (four hours thirty minutes to five hours). Two hours to the east is le Havre, which is served by ferries from Portsmouth and Southampton. Choice for most visitors depends on the convenience of the sailing times and, of course, relative costs. To the east of Normandy are the shorter, and consequently cheaper, crossings in the Boulogne and Calais area. For those who dislike ferries there is the Channel Tunnel, but this option, though quicker, is usually more expensive. From the Calais area, Arromanches can be easily reached via the new autoroutes in just over four hours, but bear in mind tolls cost up to £15. This can be reduced to about £10 by avoiding the new *Pont de Normandie*. It is worth checking all options available and making your selection of routes based on UK travel, ferry times and cost. French law requires you to carry a full driving licence and a vehicle registration document. Do not forget your passport and a GB sticker if you do not have EU number plates with the blue national identifier square.

Insurance

It is important to check that you are properly insured to travel to France. Firstly, check with your insurance broker to ensure that you are covered for driving outside the UK and, secondly, make sure you have health cover. Form E111, available from main post offices, grants the bearer reciprocal treatment rights in France, but, even so, the visitor may wish to consider a comprehensive package of travel insurance. Such packages are available from a broker or travel agent. It is a legal requirement for a driver to carry a valid certificate of motor insurance. Be warned that, without insurance, repatriating the sick or injured is very expensive, as is return of vehicles.

Accommodation

There are plenty of options ranging from hotels in Arromanches to very well-run campsites, with all other grades of accommodation in between. Arromanches has a variety of good hotels and local restaurants. Up-to-date contact details are available from the French Tourist Office, 178 Piccadilly, London W1V 0AL (01891 244 123). Further details of accommodation and travel amenities are available from the office of Calvados Tourisme, Place du Canada, 14000 Caen, France. To telephone from the UK, dial 0033, drop the 0 necessary for ringing within France, and dial 2 31 86 53 30.

Maps

Good maps are an essential prerequisite to a successful battlefield visit. Best of all is a combination of contemporary and modern maps. The *Battleground* series, of course, provides a variety of maps. However, a full map sheet enables the visitor or, indeed, those who are exploring the battlefield

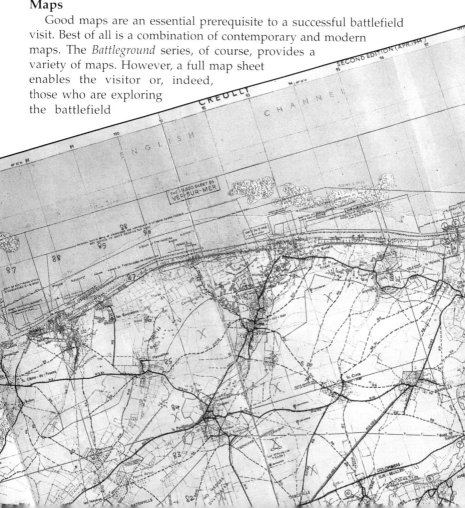

from the comfort of their armchairs, to put the battle in a wider context. Contemporary 1:25,000 map sheets (Ryes and Creully), overprinted with intelligence data, are available from the Keep Military Museum, Bridport Road, Dorchester, Dorset, DT1 1RN (01305 264066) at £4.99 each including postage and packing. They show the woods and roads as they were before the intervention of modern agriculture. Overprinted are the German positions that had been located by the Resistance and air reconnaissance prior to the battle. A number of modern map series are available in both the UK and Normandy. Most readily available in both countries are the Michelin 1:200,000 Yellow Series. Sheet 54 covers the British and US D-Day build-up and break-out battle areas and is useful for getting around the Normandy battlefield and its ports. Better still are the *Institut Geographique National* (IGN) 1:100,000 *Serie Vert* (Green Series) maps. Sheet 6, *Caen-Cherbourg-Normandie*, covers most of the Normandy battle area. Normally only available in the UK at a specialist map shop they can, however, be procured as a special order through high street book shops such as Waterstones. The *Series Vert* maps have the advantage of showing contours and other details such as unmade roads and tracks. Sheet 6 is a good compromise if you are visiting several sites and wish to use a single map. The most detailed maps, readily available in France, are the *IGN Serie Bleue* in 1:25,000 scale. The JIG area is covered by the sheet: 1512 O *Bayeux*, which includes all of GOLD Beach and Port-en-Bessin to the west. This map can normally be found in tourist shops at Arromanches. However, if you are planning your tour well in advance, large retailers in the UK can order *Series Bleue* maps, given sufficient notice.

Courtesy

The area inland from JIG Beach is mainly open farmland but many of the villages were also a part of the battlefield. Please respect private property in both open country and villages, particularly avoiding driving on unmade up farm tracks and entering non-public areas in villages. Adequate views of the scene of the action can be enjoyed from public land and rights of way. In all cases, please be careful not to block roads by careless car parking. The people of Normandy extend a genuine welcome to those who come to honour the memory of their Allied liberators. To preserve this welcome, please be courteous to the local people.

Enjoy the tour. *TJJS*, LICHFIELD

CHAPTER ONE

231 MALTA BRIGADE

General Montgomery's most experienced amphibious assault troops returned from Italy, with their Commander-in-Chief, to the United Kingdom in late 1943, after many years overseas. Sent from India and Palestine in 1939 to garrison a strategically important Mediterranean island, 231 (Malta) Brigade had endured the privations of the Island's siege, along with the Maltese people. In March 1943, the Brigade, consisting of 2 Devon, 1 Hampshire and 1 Dorset, left Malta to train at Suez for the invasion of Sicily. Spearheading Montgomery's Eighth Army in

British troops landing in Sicily.

Operation HUSKEY, 231 Brigade landed on the Sicilian coast, at 0245 hours, on 10 July 1943, successfully completing their first assault landing. Advancing from their rocky 'beach' at Marzamemi, the West Countrymen's campaign in Sicily lasted two months. Two months of hard fighting, with many casualties, took the Brigade from the south-east corner of Sicily, via the lower slopes of Mount Etna, to the Strait of Messina at the north-east tip of the island. The units of 231 Brigade won the battle honours 'Agira' and 'Regalbuto' for their assaults on strongly defended hilltop towns that dominated the surrounding area.

On 8 September 1943, 231 Brigade recorded its second assault landing by touching down on the Italian mainland. If the landing on Sicily had been against relatively light opposition, the initial stages of the subsidiary Pizzo landings, on a moonless night, were chaotic. For example, 1 Dorset's mail NCO, whose landing craft contained Rear Battalion HQ, well down the order of landing, actually led the Brigade ashore, complete with his mailbag! Nonetheless, once on the beach, having broken through the enemy's prepared positions that included concrete pillboxes, fighting inland was bitter and protracted. The cost was again significant but the Brigade and Combined Operations planners had gained further valuable assault-landing experience. After a month in action, 231 Brigade were pleasantly surprised by a hint during one of Montgomery's visits. Eighth Army News recorded:

'Monty made a speech to the Brigade. After complimenting them on their fine show, he said he hoped to take the Brigade with him wherever he went. A bit of a glum look went round the ranks. The Malta Brigade had been abroad longer than most Eighth Army men and Monty was quick to notice the reaction and added dryly, "Of course I might go to England." The effect was instantaneous. Smiles and loud cheers greeted the remark.'

Formal news that 231 Brigade were indeed to return to the United Kingdom followed shortly afterwards. Montgomery had directed that they were to join other Eighth Army veterans including 8 Armoured Brigade and 50th Division in his next campaign, although this was not immediately apparent to the soldiers at the time.

Landing in Scotland in November 1943, the Brigade's reintroduction to the cold of a British autumn was a shock for the battalions. Further shocks were in store when the West Countrymen reached their Spartan hutted camps in Essex. The grey wartime austerity of Britain was depressing but for representatives of the victorious and sun-tanned Eighth Army, the return home had some advantages! At this time, 231 Brigade formally joined 50th Northumbrian Division, losing their now informal title 'Malta' in the process. However, for the West Countrymen, being 'a part of the Northumbrian Division was a source of constant confusion for many'.

Training and Preparation

After home leave and changes of some commanders, training resumed in earnest. The King visited the Brigade in February to watch the Eighth Army veterans practising an attack and raised morale by listening to tales of action in the Mediterranean theatre. Within a short time Major 'Speedy' Bredin of 1 Dorset commented: 'Our training had already begun to acquire a fairly strong "combined operations" flavour and we realized we were "for it" again.' Early March saw the Brigade taking part in Exercise BULLOCK, where according to 1 Dorset's history, they were 'introduced to the latest mechanical methods to overcome obstacles on a hostile coast'. 'BULLOCK' was a coded reference to the specialist assault tanks of 79th Armoured Division, whose strange and novel vehicles all bore the formation sign of the bull's head.

1st Assault Brigade Royal Engineers, the heart of what eventually became 79th Armoured Division, had been raised in December 1942 following the Anglo-Canadian débâcle of the Dieppe raid. From the failure, it was apparent that assaulting a heavily defended enemy coast would require specially designed armour to lead the way ashore. Major General Percy Hobart, an early enthusiast of the tank, had been forced to resign some years earlier and had, in a peculiarly British way, become a Lance Corporal in Churchill's Home Guard. Taking off his NCO's tapes and replacing his general's crossed sword and baton, he returned to service. Taking command of 79th Armoured Division, in April 1944, Hobart, with Combined Operations assistance, studied the experience gained in the Mediterranean and at Dieppe, which he combined with an analysis of German defences on the coast of Europe. The result was a series of vehicles or 'funnies' that were manned by armoured regiments and Royal

Visit of HM the King to 1 Dorset accompanied by Brigade and Divisional staff.

Engineers, each designed to address a specific beach assault problem.

Winston Churchill's enthusiasm for 'gadgets' and technology had given impetus to the development of new weapons. He wrote in a Cabinet memo:

'This war is not however a war of masses of men hurling masses of shells at each other. It is by devising new weapons and above all by scientific leadership that we shall best cope with the enemy's superior strength.'

Major General Hobart took over development and refined designs into practical battlefield weapon systems, and, in parallel, developed tactical doctrine for effective use of his 'zoo of funnies'. He set about forging a creative atmosphere:

'Suggestions from all ranks for improvements in equipment are to be encouraged ... all ranks are to have direct access to their CO for putting forward their ideas.'

One of Hobart's first decisions was the development of the amphibious tanks. The idea of 'swimming tanks' was not new. However, in July 1943 Hobart's demonstration of launching the Duplex Drive tank from a tank-landing craft persuaded the Chief of Imperial General Staff to authorise the conversion of five hundred valuable Shermans. The key features of this 'funny' were a tall canvas screen and a pair of small propellers that could be engaged to the engine instead

Major General Percy Hobart GOC 79th Armoured Division.

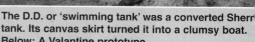

The D.D. or 'swimming tank' was a converted Sherman tank. Its canvas skirt turned it into a clumsy boat. Below: A Valantine prototype.

of the tracks. Viewing an exercise in Studland Bay, Montgomery took up the idea that the DD tanks should lead the invasion. However, with only a low freeboard, DD tanks were limited to operations in calm seas with wind strength of less than Force 4.

Most numerous of the funnies were the Armoured Vehicles Royal Engineers (AVRE). A conversion of the heavily armoured Churchill tank, the AVREs' main weapon was a Petard demolition gun that fired a 40-pound projectile, known as a 'flying dustbin', out to a range of two hundred yards. The shaped charge warhead, most accurate at a range of eighty yards, was designed to take on steel and concrete defences on the coast of France. On the back of the AVRE, a variety of obstacle-crossing devices could be carried, although most commonly carried was a *fascine* of logs for dropping in anti-tank ditches.

Completing the line-up of main equipments, were the Crab and the Crocodile. With Resistance organizations reporting that the Germans were laying more and more mines along the coast, and appreciating how slow and ponderous conventional mine clearance was, a quicker, less vulnerable, method had to be developed. Again not a new idea, the unreliable Matilda Scorpion had been used at El Alamein but Hobart produced a successful operational vehicle: the Crab or Sherman Flail, mounting a revolving drum with heavy chains to beat the ground, thus

A conversion of the Churchill Tank, the AVREs' main weapon was a Petard demolition gun that fired a 40 pound projectile, known as a 'flying dustbin'.

setting off mines and ripping up wire, as it advanced at 1½ mph. The Crocodile was a flame thrower conversion of a standard Churchill tank. Towing a four-hundred-gallon armoured trailer, the Crocodile could squirt a lance of flame, a hundred yards long, at a rate of four gallons of fire a second. The result was a fearsome weapon system, but as it was delivered only just before the invasion, few of the assault divisions knew much about the Crocodile and little use was made of flame on D-Day, despite numerous suitable targets.

At Montgomery's insistence, 50th Northumbrian Division replaced 49th West Riding Division in the assault rôle for the coming invasion. 50th Division's brigade groups, along with elements of 79th Armoured Division, were sent north to Scotland to the Combined Training Centre at Inveraray. Here they learnt the OVERLORD assault techniques. However, with the late change of tasking, 231 Brigade, as experienced amphibious assault troops, had a shortened training package. It was at this time, with a mixture of bravado and foreboding that the Brigade realized that they were, for the third time, not only to take part in an invasion but that they were also to spearhead it.

Lieutenant Colonel 'Cosmo' Nevill, Commanding Officer of 2 Devon, recalled the Brigade's arrival at Inveraray:

'There were some who wondered why all this training should be

AVRE without its gun demonstrates its agility with the help of a fascine.

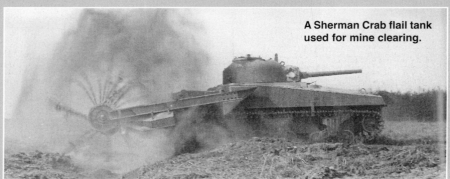

A Sherman Crab flail tank used for mine clearing.

necessary as the battalion had already plenty of experience in this particular type of warfare. After a very short time, however, we realized there was still much to learn; new weapons, new types of landing craft, new techniques had been developed and perfected since the Italy days. We found Gunners supporting assault landings by shooting their 25-pounders out of LCTs from far out to sea, with FOOs well forward in special support landing craft. This procedure appeared, to the mere infantry soldier, to be highly dangerous, but no untoward incident occurred. We heard of the amphibious DD tanks, highly secret and only spoken of with bated breath.

‘Throughout the course, emphasis was laid on the importance of close co-operation between all Services and especially with the Royal Navy. In this, we were particularly fortunate. HMS Glenroy, newly converted as an assault ship, and under command of Captain Stephen Barry RN, had just arrived in Loch Fyne. It was whispered that the Glenroy would probably carry the battalion on D-Day. ... We were the first troops to go on board and an entente was started between all ranks which grew closer and closer.’

By the end of March, 231 Brigade was based to the west of Southampton. Lieutenant Colonel Nevill recorded that low level

‘... training was a difficult problem. We were told that there would be at least six weeks available in which to get fighting fit and ready for the great day. The training areas were however few and very small, rifle ranges

The Churchill Crocodile towing a trailer filled with flame fuel which could squirt a lance of flame a hundred yards long at a rate of four gallons a second.

became progressively more difficult to obtain as more troops poured into the area. Many of us learnt for the first time that the New Forest meant literally forest, excellent for camouflage purposes, but useless for training troops in the finer points of assault landings.'

However, during this period, exercise followed exercise. Each was on a larger scale and increasingly relevant to the Brigade's D-Day tasks. The series of SMASH Exercises took the West Countrymen to their home territory. In April, many of 1 Dorset had the strange experience of conducting live firing assaults on the country surrounding their hometowns and villages along Studland Bay, while the Hampshires, during the 50th Division / Task Force G's rehearsal, Exercise FABIUS in early May, attacked the Hampshire coast at Hayling Island. In this period the Brigade,

'... saw a good deal of our affiliated armour, the Sherwood Rangers (Notts Yeomanry), an experienced armoured regiment, who had seen service in the desert and in Italy. The gunners of 90th Field Regiment were unfortunately too busy most of the time - what with trying to get the SP guns into LCTs and, having succeeded in doing that, trying to fire them from the moving craft.'

Also not properly practised was co-operation with some of the elements of 79th Armoured Division, who were concentrating on overcoming their own technical problems and developing last minute solutions to new problems. One such problem was the discovery of two peat outcrops on

Bobbin was designed to lay a mat stiffened with battens across soft going on the beaches.

Infantry 'storm ashore' during Exercise FABIUS.

JIG Sector of GOLD Beach that would almost certainly bog vehicles. Lieutenant Colonel 'Cosmo' Nevill remembered:

'Would the tanks and carriers be able to get across what appeared to be a somewhat muddy beach? ... experts were put ashore about three weeks before D-Day to test the beaches. They were found to be muddy. Experiments were immediately started on the Norfolk coast near Brancaster, where a similar type of beach exists. A gadget, known as a bobbin, was invented, which, attached to the front of a tank, would automatically unwind a coconut matting. This coconut matting was sufficiently strong to prevent the tanks and other vehicles from sticking in the soft sand and mud.'

More Visitors and the Wait

It was obvious to all that the invasion was imminent. Details of the OVERLORD plan, marked 'BIGOT TOP SECRET', were passed to progressively lower levels of command as D-Day approached. Maps of the actual coast, with bogus names, were initially circulated to allow planning while retaining some security. The D-Day secret was, however, safe as the prohibited area along the south coast and the capture and turning of German spies had both been highly effective. However, as Lieutenant Colonel Nevill recalled:

'On May 10th the three COs attended a secret conference in the brigade briefing room. The brigade commander described the plan for D-Day and gave the outline plan for the brigade. These preliminary details were given well in advance to allow time for COs to study maps, air photos, and the mass of information which was constantly coming in.

'Conference followed conference: the CO and the battalion intelligence officer were to be seen daily, coming and going, tightly clasping weighty brief cases as if their lives depended on their security, which in fact they did.'

Disrupting planning, the assault troops received more visitors. Having moved to a flat in Lord Montague's Beaulieu Palace stables to be near her husband, Diana Holdsworth recorded the aftermath of a visit to 2 Devon.

'The next visitor was Monty who was no stranger to the regulars of the 2nd Battalion. I knew of this impending visit and I looked forward eagerly to hearing all about it. David ... did not seem to be his usual cheerful self and was

not forth coming about the day... I assumed that Monty's visit had made them realize only too clearly the importance of the job they had to do and how dependent the Allies were on their success. Many years later I learned that some of the troops had booed Monty as he toured the camp.'

Private William Willis was with the Battalion during the Commander-in-Chief's supposedly stage-managed visit:

'We were ordered to close in around Monty who stood up in his car and looking down on us, spoke to us in his clipped voice that we knew well from newsreels. But the older soldiers – veterans – amongst us didn't like being talked down to in this way. There was muttering in the crowd around Monty that was silenced by glowers from the sergeant majors but afterwards as he drove around the camp he was booed and jeered by some. I suppose they didn't fancy their chances of surviving another assault landing and him telling us what he expected was the final straw.'

As on his previous visit to the Battalion in Italy, where a 'glum' was seen off by the promise of a return to England, Montgomery restored morale by ordering the Devons home on weekend leave. Shortly afterwards a very different style of visit from General Eisenhower completed the restoration of morale. Private David Powis recalled the Supreme Commander's visit:

'The General chatted to each man in turn of the front row, and even spoke through the ranks to those in the rear, jesting about their being stuck out of sight at the back, and causing laughter and comical answers to be given by them, which he shared with the addition of his own witty replies. He continued along the Brigade in a similar manner for some considerable time, then made a very impressive speech to all the 231 Brigade before responding to our salute and making his departure.

'Many said afterwards how much they liked the American General and were glad that he had been chosen to take over as Supreme Commander.'

The stage-managed three cheers of a Montgomery visit contrasted with the spontaneous applause of the assembled Brigade as Eisenhower drove off.

Shortly afterwards, as Lieutenant Colonel Nevill record-ed:

'On Monday May 29th, all invasion troops were confined to their camps. Each camp was surrounded by barbed wire, and large numbers of security police effectively stopped all contact with the outside world. At this moment, every man was let into the secret of the plan for D-Day, with the *exception of two facts – where the landing was going to take place and the actual date.... However, everyone deduced that the landing would be made in France, because we were issued with French money.'*

D Day Plans

The formation of a combined staff (COSSAC), under Lieutenant General Morgan, to plan Operation OVERLORD was ordered by Churchill and Roosevelt in January 1943 at the Casablanca Conference. The plan developed by COSSAC, as expanded, detailed and presented by General Montgomery, in April 1944, was for the Allies to land on five beaches along sixty miles of Normandy coast. The amphibious landings were to be preceded by the insertion of three airborne divisions on the flanks of the invasion area. The scale and depth of preparation required to break in to Hitler's vaunted *Festung Europa* (Fortress Europe) was of unprecedented proportions. The sketch map taken from 50th Division's D-Day Operation Order (Op O) below shows the British Second Army's assault plan.

50th Northumbrian Division, the leading formation of XXX Corps, was to land on a two-brigade frontage on GOLD Beach. 69 Brigade would land on King Sector to the east while 231 Brigade would touch down on JIG sector a mile to the west. 151 and 56 Brigades would follow the two assault brigades respectively. 50th Division was unusual in having a fourth infantry brigade under its command, as by any estimation, three brigades would have been insufficient to complete its tasks. Also under command were 8 Armoured Brigade and, for landing, 47 Commando Royal Marines. For the Division, less 231 Brigade, their objectives lay approximately eight miles inland and included Bayeux and the village of St Leger on the main Caen – Bayeux road. 8 Armoured Brigade was to push armoured patrols

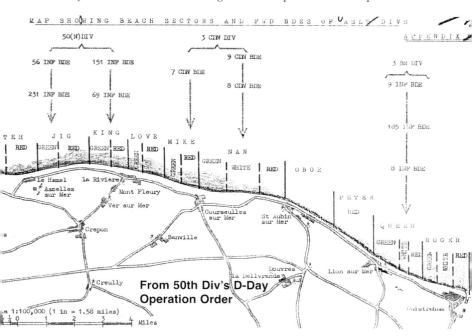

From 50th Div's D-Day Operation Order

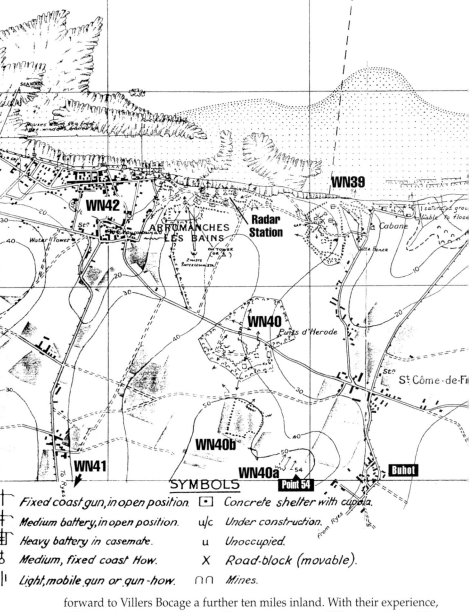

SYMBOLS

✝	Fixed coast gun, in open position.	⊡	Concrete shelter with cupola.
✝	Medium battery, in open position.	u/c	Under construction.
⊞	Heavy battery in casemate.	u	Unoccupied.
♨	Medium, fixed coast How.	X	Road-block (movable).
▮	Light, mobile gun or gun-how.	∩∩	Mines.

forward to Villers Bocage a further ten miles inland. With their experience, 231 Brigade had not only to tackle one of the most difficult sections of the Atlantic Wall but also had to link up with the Americans, almost ten miles to the west, at Port-en-Bessin. The following extract from 50th Division's Operation Order lists 231 Brigade's tasks:

'(1) **Phase 1.** *To land and secure JIG GREEN beach and establish a*

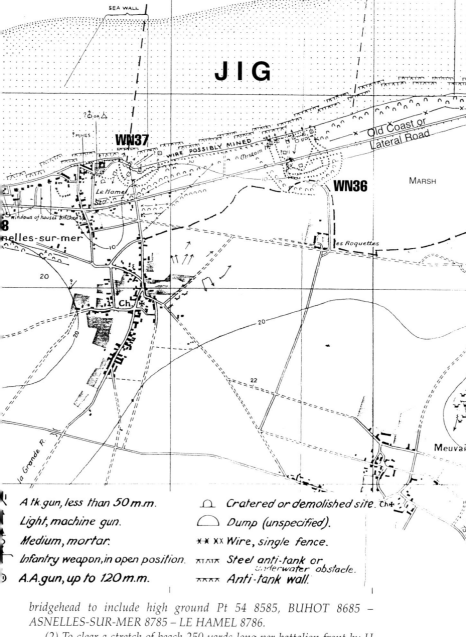

A tk. gun, less than 50 m.m.	⌂ Cratered or demolished site.
Light, machine gun.	⌂ Dump (unspecified).
Medium, mortar.	✶✶ xx Wire, single fence.
Infantry weapon, in open position.	⋊⋉⋊ Steel anti-tank or underwater obstacle.
A.A. gun, up to 120 m.m.	⋏⋏⋏⋏ Anti-tank wall.

bridgehead to include high ground Pt 54 8585, BUHOT 8685 – ASNELLES-SUR-MER 8785 – LE HAMEL 8786.

(2) To clear a stretch of beach 250 yards long per battalion front by H plus 60, to enable LCTs to beach and vehicles to pass through beach exits.

(3) To construct three tracked vehicle gaps each twenty-four feet wide i.e. two for light tracks, one for heavy tracks.

23

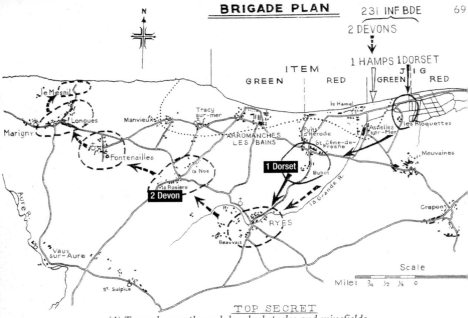

(4) To mark gaps through beach obstacles and minefields.

*(5) **Phase 2.**   To expand bridgehead to include RYES 8483 – LA ROSIERE 8284 – LONGUES 7986 – ARROMANCHES LES BAINS 8486.*

(6) [47 Commando] To capture PORT-EN-BESSIN, eight miles to the WEST of LE HAMEL.'

Landing on the JIG Beach behind 231 Brigade was 56 Brigade, who had temporarily joined 50th Division as the fourth infantry brigade. They were to take over the advance south to Bayeux, leaving 231 Brigade to concentrate on its objectives to the west.

Operation OVERLORD was to start with what, to the Germans, seemed to be routine nightly bombing raids. These raids were timed to coincide with the airborne drops. Taken from 50th Division's post-action report, the remainder of the plan was based on the following timings:

'(1) H Hour was 0725.

(2) Sunrise minus 40 [0530] – preparatory bombardment of coast defences by RN.

(3) From H minus 60 – preparatory bombardment by RN, SP [self-propelled] artillery and RAF.

(4) H minus 5 – DD squadrons arrive at firing positions on the beach.

(5) H hour – armoured assault teams land.

(6) H plus 5 – leading companies of assault battalions land.

(7) H plus 20 – reserve companies of assault battalions land.

(8) H plus 45 – H plus 60 – reserve battalions of assault brigades land.

(9) H plus 60 – H plus 90 – armoured regiment, less DD squadrons land.

24

(10) H plus 60 – H plus 120 – SP artillery lands.
(11) H plus 120 – 47 (RM) CDO lands.'

Embarkation and the Weather

The plan to embark 50th Division efficiently and quickly was, if anything, more complicated than the actual landing plan. Delivering troops, with their vehicles, stores and equipment to the correct landing craft in the reverse order to the assault required a detailed piece of, largely unrecognized, staff work by the Combined Operations planners. Despite the heavy training commitments, the Royal Navy had ensured that 97.3% of the 4,000 landing ships and craft of various types were serviceable at the beginning of June 1944, negating much expected last minute 'hot planning'. Overhead, the Royal Air Force kept enemy aircraft away from the south coast, covering 50th Division's embarkation that took place in Southampton Docks, via 231 Brigade Group's four staging areas immediately north of the city.

The Commanding Officer of 2 Devon recalled his battalion's embarkation:

'At 1030 hours on the morning of 31st May the Battalion assault group, complete with all representatives of the supporting arms, fell in for the last time. The move in MT from the camp to Southampton went without a hitch. We were driven straight to the quay alongside which HMS Glenroy *was lying ready to receive us. Tea was served to all ranks in the shed while the adjutant handed the many forms and detailed lists to the Embarkation Staff. Embarkation was completed in record time; each serial* [landing craft load] *was received on board by our Assistant Military Liaison Officer, and by the ship's Master at Arms; a Royal Marine acted as guide who not only led the serial to their correct deck, but also showed each commander the quickest way to the LCA* [Landing Craft Assault] *allotted to him. The efficiency with which the troops were received and stowed on board demonstrated the value of the close liaison which had been established with the officers and ratings of HMS* Glenroy.'

On board briefings continued with the latest air photographs being circulated and compared with special invasion overprinted maps, now complete with correct names. 'On June 3rd, we learnt that D-Day would be

June 5th subject, of course, to the weather.'

Only a few miles to the east, on the outskirts of Portsmouth, General Eisenhower had a difficult decision to make. Assembled with his staff in Southwick House, the Supreme Commander pondered '...the big question before us was the weather that would prevail during the only period of early June that we could use, the 5th, 6th and 7th'.

'We met with the Meteorologic Committee twice daily, once at 9.30 in the evening and once at 4 in the morning. The committee ... was headed by a dour but canny Scot, Group Captain JM Stagg. At these meetings every bit of evidence was carefully presented, carefully analysed by the experts and carefully considered by the assembled commanders. With the approach of the critical period the tension continued to mount as the prospects for decent weather became worse and worse.

'The final conference for determining the feasibility of attacking on tentatively selected day, 5th June, was scheduled for 4 am on June 4 ... the report we received was discouraging. Low clouds, high winds, and formidable wave action were predicted to make landing a most hazardous affair. ... Weighing all the factors, I decided that the attack would have to be postponed. This decision necessitated the immediate dispatch of orders to the vessels and troops already at sea ...

'At 3.30 the next morning, our little camp was shaking and shuddering under a wind of almost hurricane proportions and the accompanying rain seemed to be travelling in horizontal streaks. ... in such conditions there wasn't any reason for even discussing the situation.

'When the conference started the first report give us by Group Captain Stagg ... was that the bad conditions predicted were actually prevailing. ... their next astonishing declaration, was that by the following morning a period of relatively good weather, heretofore completely unexpected, would ensue, lasting probably thirty-six hours.'

At 0415 hours on 5 June, having weighed up the options, the Supreme Commander, with a look of confidence in his eyes, said, 'Ok-let's go'. D-Day was to be 6 June 1944.

The commanders and staff left Southwick House to return to their own headquarters and issue the orders for OVERLORD to begin. Now suffering the loneliness of command, General Eisenhower lifted his pen and wrote a short speech, which he was to broadcast in the event of the assault failing. In his script, he accepted total blame for failure. However, a few hours later a smiling, light-hearted and outwardly confident Supreme Commander was bidding farewell to his airborne troops.

CHAPTER TWO

FESTUNG EUROPA

German strategy in the west has been covered in considerable detail by many authors. However, in this volume, a brief resumé of German operational level plans will be followed by a more detailed examination of German aims and capabilities at the tactical level. This will be of greater relevance to those following the events that unfolded on JIG Sector of GOLD Beach.

Without doubt the much-hyped West Wall or *Festung Europa* (Fortress Europe) was not as strong as Gobbels' propaganda would have had the German people and Allies believe. However, in June 1944, the West Wall did presented a serious obstacle to Allied plans and, with every passing day, it grew stronger. So much so that, on the eve of D-Day, Churchill, cajoled (by Eisenhower and King George VI) into staying in Whitehall, rather than accompanying the invasion fleet, was wracked with doubt over the fate of his attack on *Festung Europa*.

German Operational Strategy in the West

When it became clear to Hitler that Operation Barbarossa had frozen to a halt within sight of Moscow, in late 1941, as 'General Winter' set in, he issued instructions to build a West Wall along the coast of Europe. By March 1942, this had been translated into Führer Order Number Forty. The important section read:

'The coastline of Europe will, in the coming months, be subject to the danger of enemy landings in force... Even enemy landings with limited objectives can seriously interfere with our own plans if they result in the enemy gaining a toehold on the coast... Enemy forces that have landed must be destroyed or thrown back into the sea by immediate counter attack.'

The focus of German work was to continue strengthening port defences and surrounding areas as *Oberefehlshaber* (OB) West assessed that an invading force could not be

The channel ports were heavily defended.

sustained without the use of a major port. The *pas de Calais*, with its ports and proximity to Southern England was heavily defended, and by attacking here, the Allies would have the advantages of a relatively long 'time over target' for aircraft and quick turn-around for shipping. Elsewhere along the three thousand miles of coastline from the North Cape of Norway to the Pyrenees Mountains, a thin and patchy string of defences began to take shape. However, starved of human and material resources, work on the West Wall was slow, but with Allied success in the Mediterranean and growing Allied strength in the west, Hitler issued Führer Order Number Fifty-one in late 1943:

'All signs point to an offensive on the Western Front no later than spring, and perhaps earlier.

'For that reason, I can no longer justify the further weakening of the West in favour of other theatres of war. I have therefore decided to strengthen the defences in the West, particularly at places where we shall launch our long-range war [V-weapons] *against England. For those are the very points at which the*

An isolated clifftop machine gun postion. Note the anti-aircraft gun sight.

enemy must and will attack: there – unless all indications are misleading – the decisive invasion battle will be fought.'

Along with the new orders came a new commander. At the same time as Montgomery and Eisenhower were returning from the Mediterranean, *Feldmarschall* Rommel took up the post of Inspector General of the West Wall. His responsibilities extended beyond his own Army Group B in Northern France and covered the Atlantic and the North Sea coasts. What he saw did not impress him, despite the best efforts of the Todt labour organization and its much-publicised works around the *pas de Calais*. Building on his experience of operating against Allied air superiority in the Mediterranean, Rommel assessed that he would have to defeat the enemy invasion on the beaches. To that end, with incredible vigour, Rommel set about constructing what he called a 'devil's garden' of defences. He drove his soldiers and workers hard, and, in many places, despite supply difficulties, they worked in shifts twenty-four hours a day. In six months they laid the majority of the 1.2 million tons of steel and poured 17.3 million cubic yards of concrete used in construction of *Festung Europa* and produced a 'crust' of mutually supporting defended localities. All along the coast, these localities were surrounded by over four million anti-tank and anti-personnel mines, while, on the beaches, 500,000 obstacles of various types were constructed.

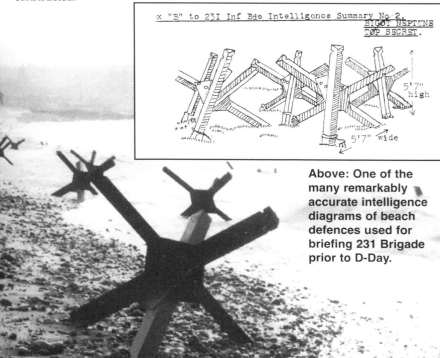

x "B" to 231 Inf Bde Intelligence Summary No 2.

BIGOT NEPTUNE
TOP SECRET.

5'7" high

5'7" wide

Above: One of the many remarkably accurate intelligence diagrams of beach defences used for briefing 231 Brigade prior to D-Day.

The tendency of dictators to prevent individuals from amassing too much power led Hitler to create an overlapping and elastic web of headquarters in the west rather than a taut chain of command. Within Commander-in-Chief (C-in-C) West's armies, *Feldmarschall* von Rundstedt and his generals did not dispute the necessity of a well-defended coastline but they could not agree how to use the scant German armoured reserves in France. With little firm intelligence to rely on, von Rundstedt, supported by the senior panzer officers, advocated the conventional military option of identifying the main enemy attack before massing reserves to counter-attack. Rommel, however, had experienced the power of the Allied air forces, and consequently, doubted the ability of the panzer divisions to assemble and make a timely move to battle while subjected to Allied air interdiction sorties. Rather than having the panzer divisions located in the centre of France, Rommel advocated forward locations, from which the panzers could intervene at the earliest stage of the Allied landings. He argued that 'penny packeting', which is contrary to the credo of any armoured commander, would in fact deliver vital armoured counter-attacks at the crucial time and place, early in the battle, while the Allies struggled to establish a beachhead. However, the senior panzer commanders, with their Eastern Front experience, disagreed, and both sides vigorously lobbied Hitler. The result was that the Führer insisted that his personal authority was required before any panzer formation was re-deployed or committed to battle. Even so, Rommel successfully used his influence to argue the case for control of three of the eight panzer formations in the west, with the remainder split between von Rundstedt and Panzer Group West. The net result was that, even if the German commanders agreed on a coherent plan for their panzers, they would still need Hitler's authority to move. It is no wonder that von Rundstedt complained, 'As C-in-C West, the only authority I had was to change the guard at my front gate'. Intelligence officer Milton Shulman, having studied the German chain of command, wrote:

> 'When the invasion began there was, therefore, neither enough armour to push the Allies back off the beaches, in the first few hours, nor was there an adequate striking force to act as an armoured reserve later on. No better design for a successful Allied landing

could have been achieved than this [German] *failure to concentrate the armour in the West along one unified and determined course.'*

The Germans Deceived

Winston Churchill wrote: 'In war-time, truth is so precious that she should always be attended by a bodyguard of lies.' Operation BODYGUARD was set up by the Allies to protect the invasion secret. BODYGUARD was one of the most comprehensive and successful deception and counter-espionage operations ever undertaken in the history of warfare. Anthony Cave Brown described the operation's aim:

'Plan Bodyguard, and the intricate special means that would be employed in its execution, had been designed for a single purpose – to enable the best and finest young men to get ashore – and stay ashore – in the first tumultuous hours of D-Day.'

Operation BODYGUARD, the Allies sought to persuade Hitler to identify a series of strategic considerations. Firstly, that the Allies thought that the bomber offensive might be sufficient to bring Germany to her knees i.e. a lack of commitment to a Second Front. Secondly, to keep the German garrisons in Norway, south-eastern Europe and the Mediterranean fixed in place and away from France. Thirdly, that the invasion would be co-ordinated to start after the Russian summer offensive and finally, BODYGUARD sought to mislead the Germans as to the size and location of the Allied invasion forces.

This last aim was the most important and with German agents either eliminated or turned, the Allies set about reinforcing the German belief that they would invade the Continent at the *pas de Calais.* Operation FORTITUDE (SOUTH) was a masterpiece of deception that was still effective well after the Allies had broken out of Normandy. Lieutenant General Morgan (COSSAC) described FORTITUDE's aim and some of the difficulties:

'... there was always the need to do everything possible to induce the enemy to make faulty dispositions of his reserves, to strive if possible to have him at a disadvantage. ... One bogus impression in the enemy's mind has to be succeeded by another equally bogus. There had to be an unbroken plausibility about it all, and ever present must

Lieutenant General Morgan

be the aim, which was to arrange that the eventual blow would come where the enemy least expected it, when he least expected it, and with a force altogether outside his calculation.'

The very core of Operation FORTITUDE was the creation of a fictitious First US Army Group (FUSAG) in south-east England under the flamboyant General George Patton. To convince the Germans that the Allies had many more divisions than they actually had available, a combination of 'special means' was used. Chief amongst these was the use of double agents, such as the Spaniard Garbo. In England, a small number of British and American signallers created FUSAG's electronic signature by simulating an army group's training and administrative radio traffic. The signallers were supported by a few genuine troops and numerous poorly camouflaged dummy tanks and landing craft and, finally, General Patton's newsworthy presence. So successful was the FORTITUDE plan that in March 1944 the *Abwehr* was reporting that FUSAG:

'... contains three armies each of three corps, each totalling twenty-three Divisions, amongst which, the location of only one need be regarded as questionable. The report confirms our operational picture.'

The Germans finally believed that there were eighty-five to ninety Allied Divisions assembling in Britain, together with seven airborne divisions. In fact, the Allies had only thirty-five divisions, including three airborne divisions. By the time D-Day came, this estimate had found its way into all the *Wehrmacht* charts and thence into its operational level plans.

Despite FORTITUDE, Hitler was becoming increasingly concerned about Normandy and urged von Rundstedt to move troops to its defence. General Warlimont of *OKH* explained, 'We generals calculated along the lines of our regular, military education, but Hitler came to his own decision, as he always did, on his intuition alone'. In this case, Hitler's intuition came too late and the picture painted by BODYGUARD and FORTITUDE was so widely accepted that there was little that could be done in the time available to redeploy significant forces in the west.

German Coastal Defences

Since Hitler issued Führer Order Number Forty in March 1942 the lower Normandy coast had been held by LXXXIV *Korps* in the form of 716th Coastal Division. With old, infirm or very young soldiers and little transport, 716th Division's slim Type 44 establishment was designed for manning static positions – in this case, a seventy-mile front between the River Dives in the east at Carbourg through to the base of the Cotentin Peninsular, for two years. However, on 15 March 1944, Hitler's intuition came into play and LXXXIV *Korps* inserted the newly organized and trained 352nd Division into the coastal defences. Thus a 'field quality'

Typical beach defences showing hedgehog and mined obstacles under construction.

An innovative re-use of captured material; here a French Renault tank turret is being installed in a purpose-built bunker as part of the Atlantic Wall defences.

division took over and consequently thickened up the defences between le Hamel and the eastern coast of the Cotentin Peninsular. Extensive regrouping of regiments, battalions and even companies took place between the 716th and 352nd Divisions, which was still incomplete on D-Day. This regrouping has led to many sources incorrectly placing the German Divisional boundary west of Arromanches rather than correctly east of le Hamel – exactly in the centre of JIG Beach. Allied intelligence did not pick up the first hints of 352nd Division's move forward until 14 May 1944 but by then it was too late to alter plans.

In a post-war debrief, 'it was discovered from General Richter of 716th Division and Colonel Ocker, the artillery commander of 352nd Division, that 726 Infantry Regiment, less one battalion, had come under command of 352nd Division from 716th Division'. The interrogator's report went on to say that '726 Regiment commanded the beach defences from the le Hamel/Arromanches area and the cliffs as far west as OMAHA'. The Germans manning the coastal fortifications in the JIG Sector were a mix of I/726 Infantry Regiment (coastal infantry) and 1st Battalion, Infantry Regiment (I/916) from the field grade division. The 352nd's Chief of Staff *Oberstleutnant* Fritz Ziegelmann stated that on his Division's fifty-three kilometre front:

> 'The former battalion sectors became regimental sectors, whereby the hitherto employed battalions of the reinforced 726 Grenadier Regiment retained their former mission, i.e. occupation of the battle installations on the coast and the formation of small attack reserves.'

Ziegelmann went on to say that he was not impressed with 726 Regiment:

> 'In taking over the sector, we were surprised that the reinforced 726th Grenadier Regiment was very backward in its training, because of the continuous supply of troops to new formations, and a

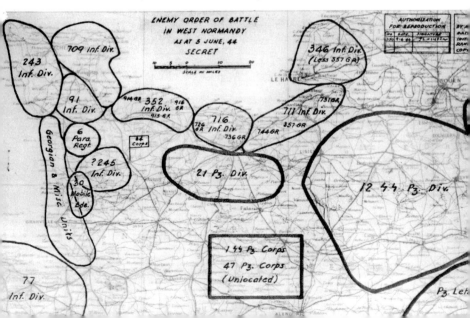

Taken prisoner on the Eastern Front, these former Soviet soldiers were pressed into German service.

lack of initiative in the officers and NCOs in training the remainder. In addition, the corps of NCOs was composed of elements which hoped to survive the war without having been under fire.'

In 726 Regiment's sector, between GOLD Beach and Port-en-Bessin, the only beaches suitable for a landing were in the area east of Arromanches stretching into 716th Division's area. It was, therefore, in this area that 726 Regiment concentrated most of its strength in largely concrete strong-points or *Wiederstandnest* (WN). I/916 took command of the lower-grade troops manning most of the coastal defences. The main effect of greatly reducing the size of regimental and battalion sectors was to produce some depth to the coastal defences. In this case, field grade infantry from I/916 Infantry, in approximately company strength, occupied field defences along the ridge (Point 54) that ran from Arromanches to Ryes. Across the broad and shallow valley of la Grande Riviere, 716th Division positioned anti-tank and machine guns on the Meuvaines Ridge, to cover this excellent route inland. Also manning positions on the Meuvaines Ridge were 716th Division's *Ost Truppen* battalion (see over page). Cosmo Nevill thought 'the prospect of forcing the way up this valley towards Ryes and Bayeux was becoming decidedly unpleasant'.

Another effect of the insertion of 352nd Division was the creation of a significant reserve under LXXXIV *Korps* control. 915 Regiment and 352nd Division's Fusilier Battalion formed the nucleus of the counter-attack force. This force initially concentrated south of Bayeux, whence they could strike at enemy landings on the beaches that came to be known as GOLD and OMAHA and against the base of the Cotentin Peninsular. However, following an exercise, supervised by Rommel in person, despite the limited

50th Div's Operation Order showing enemy positions identified prior to 352nd Div's deployment to the coast.

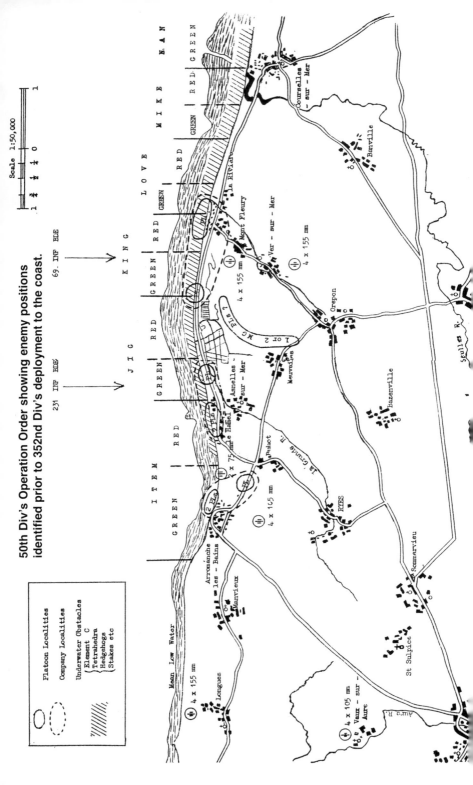

reserves for a very long divisional front, infantry companies were redeployed further forward for smaller but immediate counter-attacks. Therefore, some of 915 Regiment's infantry came under command of 726 Regiment to the north of Bayeux. In addition, the divisional assault gun battalion (1352nd with ten *Sturmgushutz*) and the anti-tank battalion (with twelve 88mm anti-tank guns) added punch to the reserves positioned between GOLD and OMAHA Beaches.

The quality of the German troops garrisoning *Festung Europa* was further reduced by the practice of taking prisoners of war from the Eastern Front and incorporating them in the *Wehrmacht*. *Ost Truppen* recruitment had followed months when:

> '*Twenty to thirty men died every night due to the combination of hours of hauling wood, generous lashing with leather whips, and bad food.*
>
> *Suddenly, in early 1942 ... Barracks were cleaned, men deloused and food became more abundant. For six weeks they were forced to take exercise so they could get their strength back. ... In May 1942 they ... discovered they were now part of four Armenian battalions which were being formed and trained to fight in the German Army.*'

By D-Day, approximately 75,000 *Ost Truppen* were serving with the German Army in France, mostly as rear area troops. *Feldmarschall* von Rundstedt was not impressed with their qualities, 'The Russians constituted a menace and a nuisance to operations'. Chief of Staff 352nd Division, *Oberstleutnant* Fritz Ziegelmann had 1,500 *Hiwis* or Russian 'volunteer' labourers to deal with. However, according to General *der Infanterie* Gunther Blumentritt, of the operational *Ost Truppen* battalions,

> '*...only four remained with LXXXIV Infantry Korps, and only two of these were committed on the coastal front. One battalion, which was especially noted for its trustworthiness, was committed on the left wing of 716th Infantry Division, at the request of this division. The other Russian Battalion was committed on the west coast of the Cotentin Peninsular.*'

441st *Ost Truppen* Battalion was positioned on the Meuvaines Ridge, in 716 Division's area, overlooking 231 Brigade's sector of GOLD Beach. The presence of a thousand Russian troops with their two hundred and seventy German officers and NCOs could have a significant impact on the course of the battle.

Beach Defences

In front of the German strong-points, the belts of wire and the minefields, lay the open expanse of JIG Beach. Not only did Rommel concentrate on organizing the *Wiederstandneste* above the high-water mark but he also oversaw the construction of a forest of beach obstacles. The

German estimate was that the Allied assault would be led by infantry, who would land at high water, when the distance across the exposed beach would be minimized. Therefore, the obstacles were set out in several rows between twelve and seventeen feet above the low-tide mark, designed to impede a landing at high water.

Much of the material used in constructing beach obstacles was scavenged from border fortifications in the occupied countries. Czech hedgehogs (jagged steel stakes), curved girders from the Maginot Line and even steel gates from Belgian forts, would, on a rising tide, be a test of the

Royal Navy and Royal Marine landing craft crew.

Chief of Staff 352nd Division *Oberstleutnant* Fritz Ziegelmann described the work his Division undertook on the GOLD / OMAHA front:

'Assuming that enemy landings would only take place at high tide, obstacles of all kinds were erected on the top part of the beach, so that their upper parts projected from the sea. "Tschechen" hedgehog defences, pile-driven stakes of metal, and concrete as well as wooden trestles were set up here and partly charged with deep water or surface mines and HE.

'During the storms in April, the mass of these obstacles were torn out and the mines exploded. It was necessary to begin again. Considering that the wood had to be cut in the Foret de Cerisy, carried at least thirty kilometres in horse-drawn vehicles (lack of fuel), had to be logged by circular saw (limited supply) and rammed by hand (which took a long time), and was particularly difficult on account of the

rocky foreground, results were surprisingly good.

'In the second half of May, the possibility of a landing at low water was discussed. The construction of obstacles to the seaward of the existing coastal defences was begun but it was impossible to build these obstacles in proper density.'

Conclusion

It is a fact that tactical, defensive positions can always be improved. However, after only two months deployed on the coast, Ziegelman summed up the state of the 352nd Division's defences in the le Hamel area:

'a. Apart from a series of small questions, the tactical organization of the 352nd Division was prepared for an enemy attack.

b. In the short time, the improvement of the battle area had made progress in spite of many difficulties, but could not be considered "good".

c. The training of the troops was continued, but not complete.'

At the operational level, after six months as Inspector of the Atlantic Wall, Rommel felt he had made significant progress. True, the German coastal defences were still a crust as the inland defences were only just being thickened by the arrivals of formations such as 352nd Division. In addition, the panzer divisions were, in Rommel's view, incorrectly located. However, the *Feldmarschall* wrote to his wife, 'I am more confident than ever before. If the British give us just two more weeks, I won't have any more doubt about it'. Finally, just two weeks before D-Day, Rommel issued a morale raising order of the day that also reflected his own growing confidence in the outcome of an Allied attack on the Atlantic Wall.

'I have expressed my deep appreciation of the well-planned and well-executed work performed in so few months.

'The main defence zone on the coast is strongly fortified and well manned; there are large tactical and operational reserves in the area. Thousands of pieces of artillery, anti-tank guns, rocket projectiles and flame-throwers await the enemy; millions of mines under water and on land lie in wait for him.

'In spite of the enemy's great air superiority, we can face coming events with the greatest confidence.'

ROMMEL
Feldmarschall
22 May 44

Despite the vast resources poured into the construction of the West Wall and Rommel's growing confidence, *Festung Europa* was in most places only a thin, hardened, crust behind which there was little depth in the German defences.

German workers run for cover as a US photo reconnaissance Lockheed F-5B makes an east to west run over JIG RED. A marsh lies behind this sector.

The western end of JIG GREEN showing Belgian Gate obstacles (foreground) and the fortified village of le Hamel (WN37) beyond.

CHAPTER THREE

THE LONGEST NIGHT

For the soldiers who were to face each other on the Normandy beaches, the night of 5/6 June 1944 was long and largely sleepless. For the Germans, their telephones started ringing shortly after midnight with reports of paratroopers dropping along the coast and hinterland from le Havre to Cherbourg. Reports were contradictory, and duty watchkeepers at divisional, corps and army level all made their own deductions and decisions on the information available. 'The paratroopers are dummies, with explosives attached' was a common report from 711th Division to the east of the Orne. However, as prisoners from the widely-scattered drop began to come in, more information was available, but defining the true extent of the landings remained difficult. An entry, amongst many similar, in 7th Army's War Diary, timed 0205 hours, reported '...further airborne landings at Pont-l'Evêque'. This report, in response to a misdrop or dummies, had reserve companies hurrying to locate and fix the enemy in position so that they could be dealt with by counter-attack. However, at

Infantry of 50th Division embarking at Southampton Docks.

PERSONAL MESSAGE FROM THE C-in-C

To be read out to all Troops

1. The time has come to deal the enemy a terrific blow in Western Europe.

The blow will be struck by the combined sea, land, and air forces of the Allies—together constituting one great Allied team, under the supreme command of General Eisenhower.

2. On the eve of this great adventure I send my best wishes to every soldier in the Allied team.

To us is given the honour of striking a blow for freedom which will live in history; and in the better days that lie ahead men will speak with pride of our doings. We have a great and a righteous cause.

Let us pray that " The Lord Mighty in Battle " will go forth with our armies, and that His special providence will aid us in the struggle.

3. I want every soldier to know that I have complete confidence in the successful outcome of the operations that we are now about to begin.

With stout hearts, and with enthusiasm for the contest, let us go forward to victory.

4. And, as we enter the battle, let us recall the words of a famous soldier spoken many years ago :—

> " *He either fears his fate too much,*
> *Or his deserts are small,*
> *Who dare not put it to the touch,*
> *To win or lose it all.*"

5. Good luck to each one of you. And good hunting on the mainland of Europe.

B. L. Montgomery
General
C.-in-C 21 Army Group.

1944.

An RAF North American B-25C overflies the invasion force heading for Normandy.

0240 hours an entry recorded that

> *'G-3 of Army Group B reports: According to Commanding General of Group West, it is not a major action...'*

Key staff officers and commanders wondered, 'Was it another false alarm?'

A Night at Sea

231 Brigade, having embarked on the 31 May 1944 at Southampton, completed their briefing at anchor in the Solent off the Newtown River. Now at last, with the latest air photographs, every man could be told the exact plan, time and date of the invasion. Over the next three days, briefings went on, at ever lower levels, in increasing detail.

Private David Powis of 2 Devon's Intelligence Section recalled the amazing detail shown on the photographs:

> *'After our battalion had boarded the ship it moved away and anchored a few miles out to sea. During that time, I can only recall one small motor-powered vessel arriving with a number of secret documents, and the very latest aerial photographs of the area we were due to invade ...*
>
> *'The photographs brought gasps of amazement and a considerable amount of admiration for the pilots who took them. They were outstandingly clear and taken from exceptionally low levels by RAF Spitfires ... They showed excellent details both when the tide was high and when it was right out.*
>
> *'... One photograph was taken at such a low level that we could clearly*

SUPREME HEADQUARTERS
ALLIED EXPEDITIONARY FORCE

Soldiers, Sailors and Airmen of the Allied Expeditionary Force!

You are about to embark upon the Great Crusade, toward which we have striven these many months. The eyes of the world are upon you. The hopes and prayers of liberty-loving people everywhere march with you. In company with our brave Allies and brothers-in-arms on other Fronts, you will bring about the destruction of the German war machine, the elimination of Nazi tyranny over the oppressed peoples of Europe, and security for ourselves in a free world.

Your task will not be an easy one. Your enemy is well trained, well equipped and battle-hardened. He will fight savagely.

But this is the year 1944! Much has happened since the Nazi triumphs of 1940-41. The United Nations have inflicted upon the Germans great defeats, in open battle, man-to-man. Our air offensive has seriously reduced their strength in the air and their capacity to wage war on the ground. Our Home Fronts have given us an overwhelming superiority in weapons and munitions of war, and placed at our disposal great reserves of trained fighting men. The tide has turned! The free men of the world are marching together to Victory!

I have full confidence in your courage, devotion to duty and skill in battle. We will accept nothing less than full Victory!

Good Luck! And let us all beseech the blessing of Almighty God upon this great and noble undertaking.

Dwight Eisenhower

Villas and houses fortified by the Germans on the coast at le Hamel. These surround Chateau Asnelles.

see into a house with a distinct view of the pictures hanging over the bed, in a house situated to the rear of the beach area we were intending to land on. ... Another photograph taken when the tide was high showed a horse drawn cart ... on the beach ... this gave us comforting information that the fairly narrow stretch of dry beach could not be mined.'

Aboard HMS *Glenroy*, 2 Devon had an important celebrity with them: Howard Marshal – the senior BBC D-Day correspondent, who had chosen to travel with '... the Middle East veterans who had been allocated the hardest task of all'. Lieutenant Colonel Nevill recorded:

'Howard Marshall's time on board was made a complete misery, but such is the penalty of fame. Any pause or dull moment was immediately overcome by "Oh get H.M. to do one of his talks over the blower [Army speak for the ship's tannoy or pipe]". He ran a quiz; he broadcast a running commentary on the ship's inter-service darts match held in the wardroom; he talked; and finally read out the inspiring messages from Generals Eisenhower and Montgomery.

'The weather steadily deteriorated. This was quite normal. Just the same thing happened on the rehearsals. At midday on June 4th a cryptic code-word was received. Captain Barry dived into the Naval instructions to find out what the code word meant; "Operation postponed for 24 hours".'

45

Presumably, Howard Marshall groaned louder than most as the delay was announced. The prospect of an indefinite delay, with the implications for security, were too awful to contemplate. However, with an improvement in the weather, another coded signal arrived and, according to Lieutenant Colonel Nevill:

> '... at 6 PM on June 5th, Force G [GOLD] (50th Division) weighed anchor and sailed west down the Solent. There was no hooting of ships' sirens; no cheering crowds as in the last war ... It was just like another rehearsal. The ships moved off in their allotted places. The Divisional Commander's ship HMS Bulolo led the field, followed by the Brigade Commander's frigate HMS Nith. We were third.
>
> '... In the distance out to sea, two immense fleets could be seen moving eastwards up the Channel. These were two more divisions linking up for the assault: truly a noble sight.'

Overhead, streams of aircraft made their way south. For those that watched from the ships, the display of airpower added to the growing confidence of the troops. However, few were able to snatch more than a couple of hours of fitful sleep. On the lower deck of HMS *Glenroy* Sergeant Willis, of 2 Devon's Battalion Headquarters, recalled that,

> 'Few of us slept well that night and about 3.30 AM we were roused for breakfast, which consisted of almost cold liver and onions and a lukewarm mug of tea'.

Lieutenant Colonel Nevill continued his account:

> 'I awoke at 3 AM and went to the bridge to see if anything was

Ships and craft of all shapes and sizes make their way through channels swept of mines.

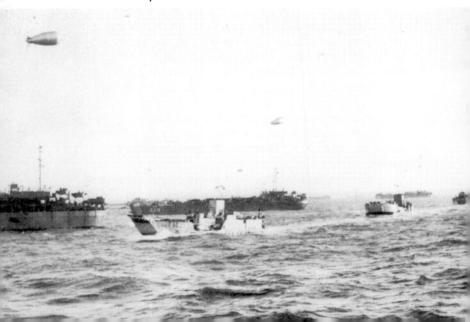

HMT Empire Spearhead with 1 Dorset's Battalion HQ LCM being lowered to starboard shortly after dawn on D-Day.

happening. There was nothing unusual in our progress, the outline of the neighbouring ships could be seen, all moving steadily at twelve knots. ... In the distance, to our right, and left front, there were signs of battle, star shells and incendiary bullets were constantly flashing in the sky, but we were still too far away for the noise of battle to be heard. This activity we presumed to be caused by the American and British airborne landings taking place according to plan.

'At dawn we anchored seven and a half miles from the coast, and there passed us a never ending procession of LCTs, LCT(R) [Rocket]*, LCT(H)* [Hedgerow]*, and all types of naval craft whose job it was to prepare the way for the landing of the infantry.'*

By 0530 hours, 231 Brigade's infantry stood in the narrow spaces between their bunks, fully kitted-up and waiting to go. At 0545, the infantry started to embark on their Landing Craft Assault (LCA). Major Mott of C Company 1 Hampshire recalled the process of leaving HMT *Empire Arquebus*:

> 'We were called up over the blower: "Serial 2042 – to your boat station – No 4 boat station – Port side – now" and I led my boatload consisting mainly of coy HQ and an assault rifle section up to our LCA. All our heavy kit had been preloaded and needed a quick check before we could report all correct. Final goodbyes and good lucks before we were lowered into a lumpy sea. ... Everything was ominously quiet.'

Second Lieutenant Holdsworth of 2 Devon recorded the embarkation of his LCA:

> 'Clambering down the side of the ship, hand over hand, gripping a suspended rope, scrambling was, for me, if not the rest of the platoon, a particularly unpleasant and frightening experience. I had no head for heights and I hated the sea. Without the military paraphernalia which we carried, it would have been bad enough. With it, it was like playing a team game of Russian Roulette. Rifles, pouches, packs and bayonet scabbards each took their part in offering the chance of a speedy death by getting caught in the ropes or on someone else. And, to further complicate our

LCAs (Landing Craft Assault) circle while others are lowered from 'mother' ships. Seen here being carried out in calm weather during excercise FABIUS, but the D-Day reality was very different.

Mixed emotions evident on the faces of these men of 1 Dorset aboard their LCA on the run-in to the beach – 30 minutes before H-hour.

individual balancing acts, the rope net which we held onto so grimly had a nasty habit of swaying against the movement of the ship and of becoming more slippery the nearer we got to the assault craft which were bobbing around like corks on the sea below us.

'... *Each of the craft carried a platoon of thirty men or their equivalent in supporting arms and staff ... In all I suppose it took some fifteen landing craft to carry the Devons to their mission.*

'*Each of the landing craft was crewed by two Royal Marines, one in the bows and one in the stern. Their job was to get us safely from HMS Glenroy to the beaches ... The Marines were highly professional in all that they did and we much admired them not only for their dual skills, naval and military, but also for their compassionate consideration for us.'*

2 Devon's Sergeant Willis recalled the next stage in the assault landing process:

'My landing craft being first off, had to cruise round and round the "mother ship' until all the LCAs were lowered from the davits and the officers and men had used the scrambling nets to get from the decks into their allotted landing craft. On board my LCM [Landing craft Mechanical – with a bow gate for vehicles] *was the CO, Lt Col Nevill, and part of Battalion HQ, the MO, some stretcher bearers, a few supporting-arms personnel as well as the CO's Jeep and the RAP Jeep.*

'The choppy sea caused sea-sickness, helped I suppose by the fear, and sitting in front of me was a stretcher bearer called Wally Hodkin who was using a bucket because he had diarrhoea and he was at the same time being sick into a bucket in front of him. The smell was frightful and combined with the very choppy sea others became sea sick – me too, eventually.'

Second Lieutenant Holdsworth continued his account:

Second Lieutenant David Holdsworth.

'The Journey from HMS Glenroy *to the beach was expected to take well over an hour – long enough for nerves and nature to demand attention. For this purpose, buckets were provided and soldiers made frequent use of these vital pieces of marine assault equipment.'*

Sergeant Willis recalled how after a prolonged period circling *Glenroy*, his battalion set off for the coast of France.

'Once all our assault craft were loaded and assembled in flight order we set off for the shore, which could now be seen a few miles away. ... There seemed to be, within sight, hundreds of small medium and large assault craft and behind us dozens of mother ships, some still lowering assault craft, and countless naval ships.'

The Wait on the Coast

The Allied deception plan was comprehensive and the bombing programme had been partly tailored to reduce German air- and ship-locating radar stations along the Channel coast to a minimum and to exploit the remaining stations for deception purposes. 'Window', or metal strips, was dropped in the *pas de Calais* to simulate a force approaching the coast in that area, and was supported by an 'electronic signature' from the fictional FUSAG, indicating that they were on the move. All this was designed to swamp German watchkeepers with so much information that they could not discern the real from the fictional, thus buying vital unimpeded time for the fleet steadily moving towards the Normandy coast.

The German defenders between le Hamel, Arromanches and Port-en-Bessin were in the centre of the invasion area and for them the call at 0200 hours to occupy their strong points was greeted with a sense of unreality. The wind was strong, scudding clouds made the night dark and, with the sound of surf on the beaches, it seemed unlikely that the enemy would come. Major Wernher Pluskat commanding a battalion of 352 Artillery Regiment in the Port-en-Bessin area recalled:

'I was woken up at about One AM by the sound of anti-aircraft fire. I telephoned the Intelligence Officer at divisional headquarters and asked what was happening and he said, "It's not clear yet, but we think US paratroops are landing to the left of us". I didn't know whether to get up or not; there had been so many false alarms and no one seemed to be taking the thing too seriously, although there was still a lot of bombing and anti-aircraft fire in the distance.

'About twenty minutes later I got a call from the Regiment and this time I was told, "It seems the invasion is beginning. You'd better get all your men to their battle stations right away". I drove in the staff car to our forward headquarters, which was a bunker overlooking the coast. It was about 2 AM by the time we got there.

Generaleutenant Kraiss, commander 352nd Infantrie Division.

'I remember feeling very excited. We'd been waiting for this thing for so long that we were glad it was coming, so we could get it over with.

'The night was very dark and a little misty. I looked out at the sea through my artillery binoculars but there was absolutely nothing to be seen. Everything was terribly quiet; there were no lights to be seen out there at all. Finally I turned round to one of the ordnance officers and said, "Just another false alarm".

'Even then, I remember having doubts. Although I couldn't see anything, it seemed unusually quiet. A little while later we heard some explosions and gunfire in the distance but there was no word from regiment or division about what was happening.'

One of the planning factors that was of most concern to 50th Division and 231 Brigade in particular was the inevitable counter-attack by the German reserves. One of Montgomery's aims in extending the invasion frontage was to dissipate German reserves

51

General Erich Marcks, Commander of LXXXIV Korps.

over a wide frontage and this is exactly what happened. 352nd *Infantrie* Division's War Diary recorded at 0300 hours:

> *'Major air landings have taken place in the Vire – low country south of Carentan; Corps reserve* [the reinforced 915 Infantry Regiment] *is immediately to march through the Foret de Cerisy to St Jean de Daye. Regimental commander is to report to Corps HQ.'*

The reserve belonging to LXXXIV *Korps*, which had planned counter-attacks into the centre of what were to be the British 50th Division's objectives inland from GOLD, were already heading away from the beach, towards the immediate threat. By 0400 hours, 915 Infantry Regiment, consisting of 2/915 Infantry Regiment and 352 Fusilier Battalion were heading west on bicycles, with support companies on commandeered French trucks, towards Balaroy. *Oberstleutnant* Fritz Zimerman commented:

> *'As was to be expected, many of the French drivers claimed it was not possible to proceed further due to engine trouble, and of course this held things up.'*

Thus, a vital force was attempting to 'punch' west under orders of *Korps* Headquarters, with inadequate transport and an ill-defined mission.

Back on the coast, through the long night, Major Wernher Pluskat was still 'standing-to' in his battle position:

> *'Hardly a word was spoken between us in the bunker, but the tension was increasing all the time. As the first grey light of dawn began to creep across the sky I thought I could see something along the horizon. I picked up my artillery binoculars and stepped back with amazement when I saw that the horizon was literally filling with ships of all kinds. I could hardly believe it. It seemed to me impossible that this vast fleet could have gathered without anyone knowing. I passed the binoculars to the man alongside me and said, "Take a look". He replied, "My God, it's the invasion".'*

CHAPTER FOUR

BOMBARDMENT
AND ASSAULT ON JIG BEACH

The firepower that the Allies had assembled to cover the run-in to the beaches and to support the assault and break-in battle was considerable. Overnight RAF bombers attacked all significant targets, such as the Longues-sur-Mer Battery. However, as the Official History records, 'it was growing light when the last of the night bombers left the target area at 0515 hours and quiet reigned on the coast for a few minutes'.

Major Werner Pluskat, at his artillery command post on the coast near Port-en-Bessin, had spotted the invasion force and,

'... called Major Block, the intelligence officer at divisional headquarters. "There must be ten thousand ships out there," I told him. "It is unbelievable, fantastic..." Block said, "Look Pluskat, are you really sure? The Americans and the British together don't have that many ships." I just said, "For Christ's sake, come and look for yourself," and then, because of the disbelief in his voice, I said, "To hell with you," and threw down the receiver.

'Suddenly we saw planes approaching from the sea and they began bombing the beaches. The bombing continued for a solid forty minutes. There were thunderous explosions all around us, but we were relatively safe behind the thick walls of the bunker.

'We watched, absolutely petrified, as the armada steadily and relentlessly approached. It was an unforgettable sight; I don't think I had ever seen anything so well organized and disciplined. At about five o'clock in the morning [0525 hours] the fleet began manoeuvring in front of us and I realized that the battleships were getting ready to fire. I telephoned Bock and asked permission to fire. He replied, "No, no. We're too short of ammunition. No gun must fire until troops are nearing the beaches."

'To my horror and amazement, I could clearly see the guns of the fleet being elevated as they swung slowly round to point in our direction. A lilac-coloured flare was fired. Then the bombardment from the sea began. The shells screamed like a thousand express trains and all seemed to be converging on our position. One of the first shells hit the base of our bunker and literally shook it. I was thrown to the ground and my binoculars were smashed. There was dust, powder, dirt and splinters of concrete all over the place and, although many of the men were shouting, no one seemed to be hurt. The firing continued, shell after shell pounding the bunker.

'It was unbelievable to me. I was completely dazed and unable to speak

A Royal Navy destroyer (HMS Glasgow) engages a coastal battery and experiences some near misses during the morning of D-Day.

and all the time the bunker was shaking. I remember looking at my watch. It was seven o'clock. All my communications had been cut except for an underground cable to the chateau where the divisional headquarters was. This telephone kept ringing with demands for a report on the situation. I picked up the phone and someone said, "Please give an exact location of where the bombs are falling." I shouted back, "For God's sake, they're falling all over. What do you expect me to do, go out and measure the holes with a ruler".'

Working from west to east, the French cruiser *Montcalm,* supported by British and American destroyers, bombarded the Port-en-Bessin area, including Major Werner Pluskat's command post. Further to the east, HMS *Ajax's* eight six-inch guns engaged the Longues-sur-Mer Battery, while *Argonaut* shelled the Vaux-sur-Aure Battery position and *Emerald* the enemy positions immediately inland of Arromanches. The Dutch gunboat *Flores* took on a cleverly sited two-gun position on the cliffs overlooking JIG Beach at Cabane (*Wiederstandneste* 39 [WN39]). Commander Kenneth Edwards summarized the overall effect of the opening phase of the bombardment:

'Despite the virtual invulnerability of the bigger batteries and the fact that the enemy had moved many of his gun positions, the combined effect of the air and the first part of the naval bombardment had the effect of silencing, temporarily at least, nearly all the fixed German batteries. This was done, according to plan, just before the leading ships came within range. It is true that a certain amount of intermittent trouble was experienced with some batteries but each time they opened fire they were engaged again by ships with such accuracy that they again lapsed into silence.

'As soon as the more formidable of the German coastal defences had been neutralised, the cruisers of the bombarding force turned their attention to the other German defences, such as pillboxes, redoubts, anti-tank defences, and machine-gun posts, while the heavier ships stood ready to re-engage any heavy German battery which might reopen fire. The cruisers were, of course, able to operate much closer inshore than the heavy ships and could therefore bombard the enemy positions at short range with direct observation from the ships. It was this [second] phase of the naval "fire plan" which saw to it that the troops and tanks of the first waves of the assault were not held up by such obstacles as had been encountered undamaged at Dieppe.'

Supporting the cruisers of Bombardment Force K off GOLD were no less than fourteen destroyers of the 25th Destroyer Flotilla, reinforced by destroyers of 21st Flotilla and the Polish ship *Krakowiak*. They approached JIG Beach just ahead of the assault force. The four Hunt class destroyers engaged *Wiederstandnest* 36 at les Roquettes, while three Fleet class destroyers were to suppress enemy positions in le Hamel. Commander Edwards continued his account with details of the third phase of the naval fire plan:

'This was the "drenching" of the beaches and their immediate approaches from landward by the guns of the destroyers and the LC(G)s [Landing Craft (Gun) mounting 4.7-inch guns]. Destroyers mounting 4.7 and 4-inch guns and a great collection of other craft ranged up and down the beach, literally "drenching" every square yard of them from water line to vegetation line with high explosive shells. Behind that curtain of fire the landing craft laden with assault troops made for the beaches.'

One of the specially developed fire support craft was the rocket-firing conversion: the Landing Craft Tank (Rocket) (LCT[R]). Four of these craft, each mounting 800 – 1,000 twenty-nine-pound high explosive rockets, fired at a range of 3,500 yards, were allocated to 231 Brigade's Assault Group G1.

Landing Craft Tank (Rocket) delivers a salvo of 5-inch rockets during the invasion.

Landing Craft
BRITISH AND AMERICAN

L.C.P. (L)
LANDING CRAFT
PERSONNEL (LARGE)

L.C.P.
LANDING
(RAMPED)

L.C.A.
LANDING CRAFT ASSAULT

L.C.S. (M) Mk. I
LANDING CRAFT
SUPPORT (MEDIUM)

L.C.S. (
LANDING
SUPPORT

L.C.T. (5)
LANDING CRAFT
TANK

L.C.M.
LANDING
MECHANI

L.C.T. (4)
LANDING CRAFT TANK

L.C.M.
LANDING
MECHANI

L.C.T. (3)
LANDING CRAFT TANK

L.B.V.
LANDING
VEHICLE

L.C.F. (3)
LANDING CRAFT FLAK
(THREE)

One of three contemporary training posters intended to familiarize troops with the landing craft in use on D-Day.

Capable of delivering a very heavy weight of fire in a matter of seconds, at H-10 and H-4 minutes, LCT(R)s suffered the drawback of only having one shot before having to withdraw to rearm. Trooper Joe Minogue of the West-minster Dragoons, in one of the leading LCTs, had a good view of the LCT(R)s in action.

'The amazing thing to us was these rocket ships they had got. They were tank landing craft with a vast number of down spouts sticking over the side at an upward angle. The ships turned lazily to one side and fired a vast number of rockets at the beach, then man-oeuvred to fire the other side.'

Battle preparation. A soldier from 231 Infantry Brigade adjusts the gas regulator on his Bren Gun barrel.

Also with only one shot were the Landing Craft Tank (Hedgerow) (LCT[HR]). These craft fired salvos of three hundred and eighty twenty-four or sixty pound high-explosive spigot bombs, also designed to 'drench' the German defences with fire to cover the landing of LCTs carrying the Funnies at H-Hour. Also covering the run-in to JIG were the LCT (Support). These were standard tank landing craft each adapted to carry two of the Army's self-propelled guns, with sufficient ammunition to fire on the move inshore and to come into action promptly once on dry land. 90 and 147 Field Regiment were to open fire on the beach defences at H-35 minutes, at a

JIG Green east of le Hamel, where the Hampshires landed.

range of approximately 11,000 yards from the beach, checking fire at H-Hour in preparation for their own landing at H+60 minutes. For the bombardment on JIG Beach, 147 Field Regiment had an allocation of 3,800 rounds. Sergeant Major Jack Villader Brown recalled:

> 'Everybody opened up, the noise was horrific, it was ear shattering. In that running shoot, the guns got so hot the blokes could hardly handle them. Grease was running out of the breech-blocks and the empty cartridge cases were being thrown over the side. Each gun fired between 150 and 200 rounds – as soon as one's gone, you put another one in. We didn't have time to be afraid, you don't get time to think.'

However, because the launch carrying the artillery Forward Observation Officer broke down, the significantly strong position at le Hamel, which enfiladed JIG Beach, was not engaged as planned. Instead, the guns joined in the shoot on WN 36. This early failure, compounded by earlier misses by the Air Force, led to the assault infantry facing unsuppressed and very lively enemy in well prepared positions. But elsewhere, the bombardment on JIG Beach was effective and did much to destroy the German morale and field defences. However, even a direct hit on a concrete casemate, by all but the heaviest shells, did little damage – other than to the nerves of the occupants.

H-Hour, 0725 6 June 1944

Aboard his LCA, Lieutenant Holdsworth peered cautiously over the bow towards France.

> 'Well astern of us now lay the war ships, the troop ships and all manner of other strange naval craft stretching from east to west as far as the eye could see. Overhead shrieked an endless stream of aircraft on their way to bombing or machine-gun raids on the Germans, or returning from them. There was so much to see and so much noise that it was difficult to think any further ahead than our immediate requirements.
>
> 'As the coastline of Normandy grew more distinct, we could see great curving spouts of water being thrown up in our path by exploding enemy shells. By contrast, we could not only see but also hear rockets and shells being hurled into the enemy positions.'

However, not all was going to plan. The DD Shermans of the Sherwood Rangers were to have been launched from their LCTs about 3,000 yards from the coast but the force six wind had whipped up waves that would swamp the fragile canvas screens. Consequently, they were not launched. The loss of all but a few of the DDs on the run-in to OMAHA indicates that this was a sound decision. An entry in 231 Brigade's war diary recorded that 'The eight LCTs carrying the DD tanks, having just returned through failure to float the tanks are passing us going seaward.' The LCTs carrying Sherwood Rangers' DD tanks, joined the rear of 231 Brigade's initial assault force, eventually carrying out a 'deep wade' of five hundred yards to the shore. The two DD squadrons actually landed at H+35 on the border between JIG Red and KING Green, behind the Rangers' ordinary Sherman squadrons that landed at H+90. The failure of the DD tanks to land at H-5 was to have a profound effect on 231 Brigade's landing, starting with a lack of tank support to the assault engineers at H-Hour.

Another departure from the plan, however, had beneficial consequences. The assault force found itself too far inshore during the naval fire plan and, if they had continued, was in danger of running into the shells of the final phase of the Navy's fire plan. This necessitated the flotillas attempting to 'mark-time' for ten minutes. This, however, was easier said than done. With a tight formation and the strong current, the craft were sent half a mile to the east, away from strongly defended le Hamel towards a sector of the beach behind which lay a marsh. This part of the beach was, consequently, not as well-defended and enabled at least a part of 231 Brigade to get ashore relatively easily.

Without the DD tanks, the invasion was to be led by the assault teams from 79th Armoured Division. Landing at H-Hour, the Funnies were formed into six teams of specialist armour drawn from 82 Squadron, 6 Assault Regiment RE and B Squadron The Westminster Dragoons. Each team consisted of six vehicles: two Churchill AVREs mounting Bobbin and Roly Polly (to get across the peat strip), two Crabs (Flails), an AVRE

The planned breaching locations for the 79th Armoured Division's assault teams.

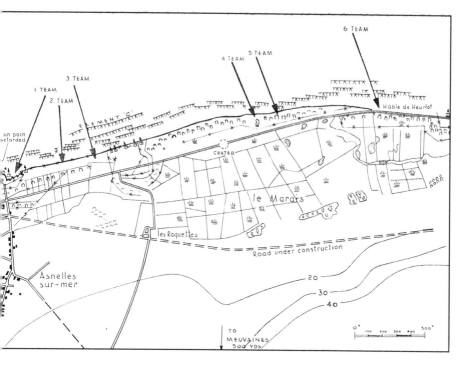

Three vehicles of an assault team knocked out on JIG, including a Crab, a Bobbin and an AVRE.

View towards le Hamel from the area of WN36. The sea wall is modern.

le Hamel East
77mm casemate

Arromanches

carrying a fascine and another vehicle suitable for each team's task. These options included armoured and unarmoured bulldozers, additional AVRE variants (such as SGB ramps) or another flail tank. Landing from the same LCTs were naval clearance engineers who were to blow obstacles below the waterline and ninety Royal Engineers from 73 Field Squadron who were to clear beach obstacles. In the event, this task was complicated by the large waves and the fact that the westerly wind had 'ponded' the tide in the channel and, therefore, the sea level at H-Hour was considerably higher than had been planned for.

Aboard one of the six LCTs bearing the assault teams, with nothing ahead but the enemy, was Trooper Minogue of B Squadron, Westminster Dragoons:

'You can imagine the position with five of us in the tank crew, each man with his own thoughts, each dependent on the other. ... We had just one job really, that was to get off the landing craft and once we had reached the high water mark on the beach we had to begin flailing – beating mines with chains at the front of the tank – and keep going until we reached the road. Then we were to turn right and rendezvous in the village of le Hamel.

We saw the first couple of tanks go off, then the third one. We were the fourth tank off the landing craft and we were very apprehensive about being in the water. I think the driver of the tank was a bit more apprehensive than the rest of us because he blew part of the waterproofing a little before he should have done and we thought, "Oh, this is it. We've been hit, this is the end of it".

I was the gunner and I only had a forward view but I could see that the three tanks in front of us were not doing too well. The first tank [AVRE] had stopped because its commander was killed, the second tank [AVRE] had been a bit too close to him and had slewed to the right and hit a clay patch on the beach and bogged. The tank [flail] behind him was hit in the side. I saw the crew busily scrambling out.'

The flail was in fact the second casualty to enemy action. A captured Polish 77mm anti-tank gun, mounted in a massive casemate on the sea front at le Hamel, had earlier hit the LCT carrying Number I Team. The craft slewed sideways across the beach and was unable to discharge its vehicles until later. From the first moment of the landing, this 77mm gun was to be a problem. Brigadier Stanier explained that, in addition to the artillery failure:

'The air strike NOT only missed le Hamel but most important the pill-box at the east end which caused all the trouble ... owing to insufficient liaison between ground and air, the RAF had not realized the importance of the target. ... All contact with aircraft had to be made through the RAF representative at divisional HQ and thence to RAF HQ at Uxbridge.'

However, with the troops planned to be closing in on le Hamel there was no chance to rectify the situation. Brigadier Stanier went on to say that the 77mm,

> '... was completely defiladed from the sea by massive concrete walls and it had a magnificent enfilade shoot along the beach. Its low profile and the way it blended into the background meant that it was not bombarded from the sea.'

However, of the five teams, Numbers II, IV, V and VI were successful in getting at least one flail through to the lateral road that ran across the marsh, just behind the narrow belt of dunes. As Brigadier Stanier commented:

> 'This was only done at a considerable cost in AFVs, all victims of the 77mm in the casemate. The Bobbin and Roly Polly AVREs were all unsuccessful in laying their mats except the Bobbin AVRE in VI team.

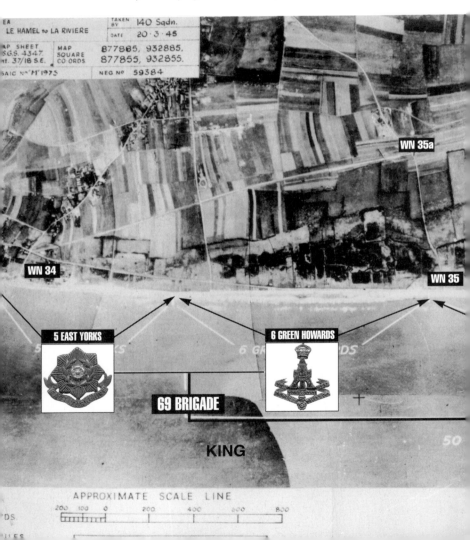

EA LE HAMEL to LA RIVIERE		TAKEN BY	140 Sqdn.
		DATE	20·3·45
AP SHEET SGS. 4347 nt. 37/18 S.E.	MAP SQUARE CO-ORDS	877885, 932885. 877855, 932855.	
SAIC N° M° 1975		NEG N°	59384

WN 35a

WN 34

WN 35

5 EAST YORKS

6 GREEN HOWARDS

69 BRIGADE

KING

50

APPROXIMATE SCALE LINE

200   100   0   200   400   600   800

Fortunately the beach made better going than expected and so this failure did not hold up operations very seriously. Failures were due to bogging of inexperienced crews, and to fire from the 77mm, which accounted for most of them.'

H+5 – 0730 Hours 6th June 1944

A Royal Marine commanding an LCA recalled, as his craft approached the beach, running in on the waves:

'The soldiers were so glad to get off the landing craft to escape the seasickness that by the time we reached the beach, they would have gone anywhere!'

Following five minutes behind the Assault Teams, little more time than it would take for the Funnies to disembark, were 231 Brigade's leading infantry battalions, 1 Hampshires on the right and 1 Dorsets on the left. The

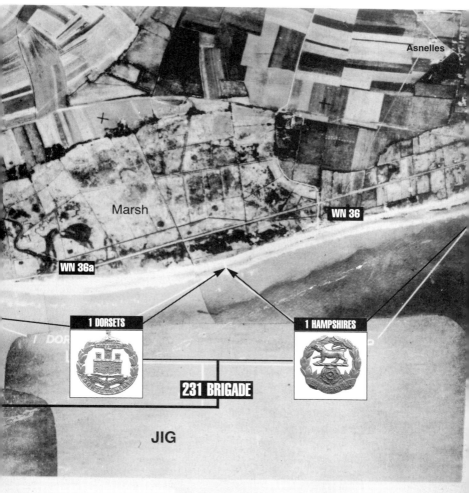

Dorsets had been due to assault the strong point at les Roquettes (WN 36) and the Hampshires the coast immediately east of le Hamel, where the incomplete concrete sea wall ended. Major Mott recalled his responsibilities during the final run-in to the beach:

> 'We were told about the preliminary bombardment and that we should find the smoke and dust blotting out all recognizable features before we landed, so, although an ML would guide us near the landing site, I was responsible for guiding the first wave to the right spot. I studied air photographs of the beaches and picked out a large log at the right point. ... Soon our ML had done her work and turned away, leaving us to run into the shore which we could see, but in no detail. And still no fire came back. From the air photograph, I had picked out a prominent log, above high water mark to the east of le Hamel. For a while I could not even see this.
>
> After a bit I picked out a fallen tree slightly to our left and told our coxswain to steer for it. As we neared the water's edge, the bombardment lifted and some shells and mortar bombs began to fall in the water among the craft, nothing really close to us. Ahead we could see LCTs disgorging tanks and the underwater obstacles were high and dry, being tackled by intrepid Sappers.'

Major Mott had confused a fallen tree with his chosen log, which took him ashore further east than intended. Navigation difficulties and the current, as has already been explained, combined with this navigational error to set the assault craft up to half-a-mile to the east of their landmark. 1 Hampshire landed opposite les Roquettes, while the Dorsets landed on a lightly-defended beach further east on RED on the boundary of JIG sector. It is the considered opinion of Brigadier Stanier and his brigade that this was '... entirely fortuitous as the defences of le Hamel were still largely intact following the naval [artillery and air] bombardment'.

Approaching JIG GREEN, Private Hooley, a radio operator in Headquarters A Company, 1 Hampshire recalled:

> 'Overhead there was a continuous whiz of naval shells homing in on their targets to soften them up for us. We were soon within range of enemy mortars, a weapon we had grown to respect, and we could hear the sharp crackle of machine-gun fire. We had the word to get ready and tension was at its peak when the ramp went out. I was with the second in command of the company, a captain. He went out with me close behind. We were in the sea to the tops of our thighs, floundering ashore with other assault platoons to left and right of us. Mortar bombs and shells were erupting in the sand and I could hear the burp of Spandau light machine-guns through the din. There were no shouts, only the occasional cry as men were hit and went down.
>
> 'The beach was filled with half-bent running figures and we knew from experience that the safest place was to get as near to Jerry as we could. A

A Sherman flail knocked out on JIG Beach, victim of the 77mm.

An infantry aid post on JIG using the bulk of a knocked out AVRE as cover from fire coming from le Hamel.

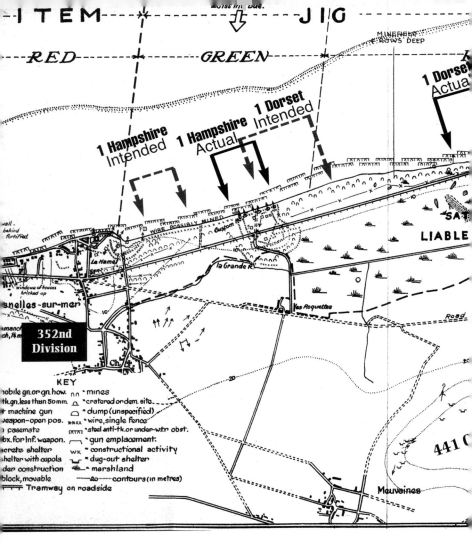

near one blasted sand over me and my radio went dead, riddled with shrapnel. A sweet rancid smell, never forgotten, was everywhere; it was the smell of burned explosive, torn flesh and ruptured earth.

High up on the beach a flail tank was knocked out, I saw B Company's Headquarters group take cover behind it just as a shelled scored a direct hit on them. They were gone in a blast of smoke out of which came cart-wheeling through the air a torn shrieking body of a stretcher bearer with the red cross on his arm clearly discernible.'

Following behind the knocked out flail was Trooper Minogue in the second flail of Number Two Team:

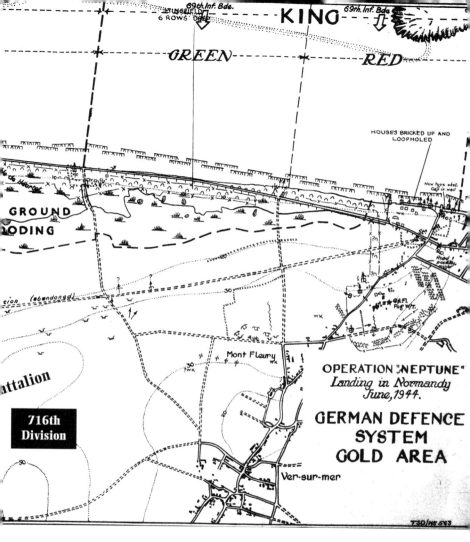

OPERATION "NEPTUNE"
*Landing in Normandy
June, 1944.*

**GERMAN DEFENCE
SYSTEM
GOLD AREA**

716th
Division

'As I began a traverse to the left I saw a pillbox here and there but I wasn't sure if anything was coming from it or not. Then as the turret came back towards the sea I could see the infantry coming ashore. It was a bit like a cartoon, a bit unreal. I suppose there must have been a couple of machine guns raking across the beach. You could see the infantrymen getting into the water from the small landing craft, some chest-deep, some waist deep and they began to run across the beach and suddenly you'd see the odd figure falling here and there.

It wasn't a matter of a whole line of men going down; it seemed as though just one in five, or a small group might go down. A chap would be

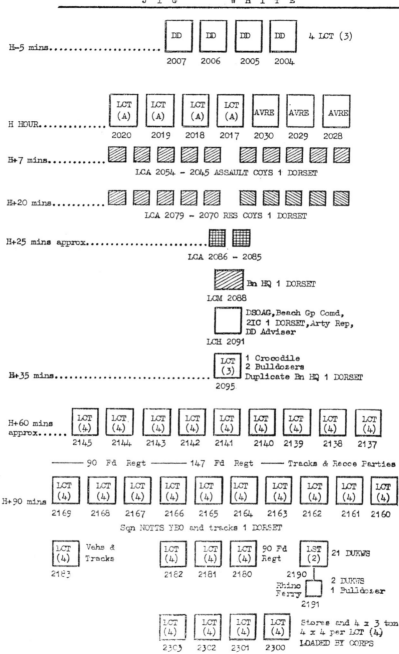

JIG WHITE

H-5 mins........................ DD 2007 DD 2006 DD 2005 DD 2004 4 LCT (3)

H HOUR.............. LCT (A) 2020 LCT (A) 2019 LCT (A) 2018 LCT (A) 2017 AVRE 2030 AVRE 2029 AVRE 2028

H+7 mins............ LCA 2054 – 2045 ASSAULT COYS 1 DORSET

H+20 mins........... LCA 2079 – 2070 RES COYS 1 DORSET

H+25 mins approx........................ LCA 2086 – 2085

Bn HQ 1 DORSET
LCM 2088

DSOAG, Beach Gp Comd,
2IC 1 DORSET, Arty Rep,
DD Adviser
LCH 2091

H+35 mins............................... LCT (3) 2095 1 Crocodile
2 Bulldozers
Duplicate Bn HQ 1 DORSET

H+60 mins approx...... LCT (4) 2145 LCT (4) 2144 LCT (4) 2143 LCT (4) 2142 LCT (4) 2141 LCT (4) 2140 LCT (4) 2139 LCT (4) 2138 LCT (4) 2137

———— 90 Fd Regt ———— 147 Fd Regt ———— Tracks & Recce Parties

H+90 mins LCT (4) 2169 LCT (4) 2168 LCT (4) 2167 LCT (4) 2166 LCT (4) 2165 LCT (4) 2164 LCT (4) 2163 LCT (4) 2162 LCT (4) 2161 LCT (4) 2160

Sqn NOTTS YEO and tracks 1 DORSET

LCT (4) 2183 Vehs & Tracks   LCT (4) 2182 LCT (4) 2181 LCT (4) 2180 90 Fd Regt LST (2) 2190 21 DUKWS
Rhino Ferry 2191 2 DUKWS
1 Bulldozer

LCT (4) 2303 LCT (4) 2302 LCT (4) 2301 LCT (4) 2300 Stores and 4 x 3 ton
4 x 4 per LCT (4)
LOADED BY CORPS

The original landing diagram for JIG used by 231 Brigade. For the 'eyes only' of officers cleared to have sight of the BIGOT Top Secret D-Day plans.

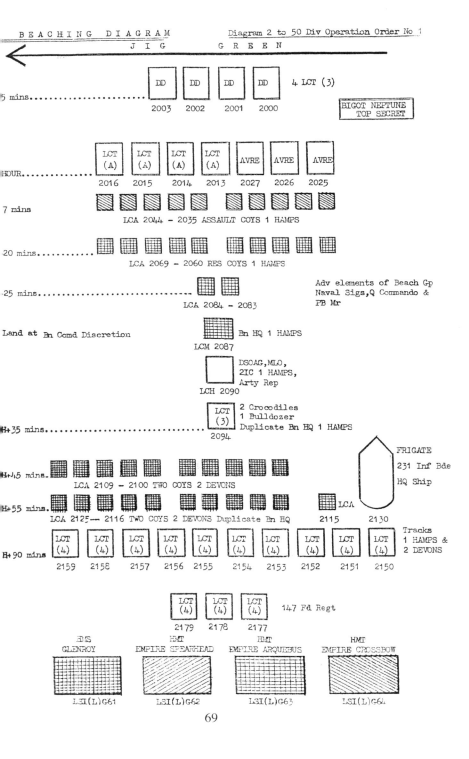

lying doubled up on the beach and some people would run past him and then a couple of his mates might get hold of the epaulettes on his battledress and drag him forward to the shelter of the sand dunes.'

The 'pillboxes on the left' were a part of the German *Widerstandnest* at les Roquettes (WN36) that the Hampshires' assault companies had unexpectedly found themselves astride. 231 Brigade Intelligence Summary Number 2, issued in early May, described the enemy position.

'This is surrounded by two wire fences, each six to eight feet thick, approximately 30 yards apart. Inside this outer ring is another barbed wire fence, twelve to fifteen thick. There is no wire on the seaward side of the strong point.

'The coastal mine belt forms a half circle around the landward side of the strong point, and continues to the EAST and WEST. It is thought probable that the space between the outer belts of wire may contain anti-personnel mines.

'The strength of the strong point is thought to be approximately one platoon strong. It consists of five pillboxes, two of which are under construction [complete by D-Day], and probably two pillboxes at the X-rds. There are also three weapon pits [field defences] covering the beach, and one facing EAST – probably to cover the minefield. Within the area of the strong point is a position for one infantry gun, and an A Tk gun is sited near the two pillboxes at the X-rds.'

The 'drenching' naval and air bombardment extensively damaged WN 36. The wire had been torn, communication trenches and field defences largely flattened and it is assumed that the many of the mines had been exploded by the bombardment, as casualties from mines in this area were light. Despite the bombardment, the concrete positions were still active, as Private Holley recorded: 'We got across the beach to where a *Spandau* from a pillbox to our left flattened us until it was silenced'.

The other side of WN 36 (to the east) was B Company led by Major Mott, whose exhortation for his troops to 'Get up them beaches' was cut short as he disappeared into a underwater hole. Having surfaced and regained his footing, he recalled that:

'We could see tanks [AVRE] and a flail tank ahead of us and toiled on, walking rather than running. I found myself in the lead, going between obstacles. ... I was keen to get off the beach, which was starting to become less safe. At last we reached a thin belt of wire. We paused for a moment and joined 11 Platoon and told a man with the wire cutters to get busy and the tape man to follow. The latter rather slowly and crookedly went forward, paying out the tape to mark a safe route through a field of reeds some five feet high. ... I got my men away from the beach, but some of Coy HQ crouched down behind a tank and got a direct hit...

As soon as the tape man was well out in front, we followed in a long

70

Major General Graham and the Staff of 50th Division observe the landings from the deck of HQ Ship, HMS Bulolo, early on D-Day.

snake. Only a direct hit could have done much damage in the reeds. There were other snakes on either side and we got safely to the hedge which should have been La Grande Riviere some eighteen feet wide. But it wasn't.'

Major Mott realized that he had landed too far to the east. Meanwhile, 231 Brigade's post-operational report recorded that

'The two [Hampshire] *reserve companies, C and D, landed at 0740 hours, and also came under withering MG fire from pillboxes, which the tanks that landed at H-Hour, were ineffectively trying to neutralise. 88mm fire from guns sited well inland* [Point 22, the Meuvaines Ridge to the east and Puis d'Herode to the west], *which had followed the invasion craft inshore, now concentrated on the troops collecting on the beach.'*

Coming ashore in 1 Hampshire's second wave was Major David Warren, who led C Company up onto dunes at the back of the beach:

'About twenty British troops could be seen fighting near some pillboxes at the edge of Les Roquettes. The enemy were not offering much opposition and although some continued to fight on many gave themselves up to the troops running up the beach from their craft.

'With this platoon was the second in command of A Company who said that his company had landed well down to the eastern end of the beach and that the two other platoons were last seen working their way towards le Hamel against stiff opposition.'

German *Grenadier* Hubbne recalled the initial battle on the beaches:

Les Roquettes (WN36) shown in a marked intelligence air photo issued for the briefing of 1 Dorset.

'On the command we opened fire. Then we saw lots of strange looking tanks coming off the boats and I thought, "My God, if they get to us we're finished". Some of the tanks sank in the sea, but others rolled up the beach and we could not stop them. But we heard our anti-tank guns firing and three of the tanks were destroyed. The others were shooting at us and all kinds of débris were flying about. I felt something hit my forehead and blood flowed, so I wrapped a handkerchief around my head. Then there was a horrible crash and our bunker filled with smoke. I fell down and saw bodies and thought it was the end. Then the Feldwebel came and helped me up and together we started firing again. We used an undamaged machine-gun, but after a short time we heard a lot of noise behind us and realized the enemy tanks and infantry were in our rear.*

'Suddenly there was a lot more noise and the whole bunker collapsed. A tank had come up and fired a heavy charge that really destroyed everything.'

This 'heavy charge' was fired by an AVRE of Number Three Team that 'dealt with' sufficient enemy-held casemates to enable the Hampshires to break into WN 36. After a short fight, A and B Companies captured the defenders, including Grenadier Hubbne, who was relieved to be well on his way to a PoW camp in England by mid-afternoon.

Before WN 36 could be considered cleared, Lieutenant Colonel Nelson-Smith, 1 Hampshire, who had insisted on landing immediately after his assault companies, arrived with his tactical headquarters, which included the commander of his affiliated battery of 147 Field Regiment RA, Major RB Gosling, who wrote:

'... a swarm of angry bees buzzed just above our heads; our Hampshire comrades, war-experienced, recognized German heavy machine-gun fire and ran forward. In front of us the sand furrowed and spurted from Spandaus firing down the beach in enfilade on fixed lines from le Hamel. The Colonel shouted to us to lie down, but the wet sand was unattractive, so we sprinted for the cover of the dunes fifty yards ahead.

German defenders manning a casemate.

A unique series of photographs taken by Captain Henden with an illegal camera, showing 1 Dorset's run-in to JIG GREEN.

The 'Funnies' are already ashore with RE and RN clearance teams.

Almost there. A drowned AFV can be seen and the sand dunes at the back of the beach where they will soon be finding shelter.

'Some mortar bombs and 88mm shells were falling and one of the former landed just behind the CO and I, smashing one of his arms and filling my leg with shell fragments. We managed to make it to the dunes and flung ourselves in a depression in the sand. Intermittent bombs and shells continued to fall and machine-gun fire swarmed through the reeds above our heads. We laid very flat and still. ... After a few minutes, German fire seemed to have switched down to the beach again [to engage another flight of landing craft] *and I crawled up the dune to peer over the other side. Horrified to see a German twenty yards away, I fired my revolver in his general direction and hastily slid back. A Hampshire corporal lying near me, already wounded, knelt up to look over the dune and was at once shot through the chest by a sniper.'*

With the CO and battery commander both wounded, the Hampshire's command group was paralysed at a crucial moment. Eventually the second-in command, Major Martin (Dorset Regiment) came to take over but was killed shortly after arriving at Tac HQ. It was some time before a message could be got through to Major David Warren, with C Company, to take over command and even longer for him to extricate himself from his own battle and reach Tac HQ. During this time, the remaining company commanders pushed on to their objectives as planned.

Meanwhile, on 231 Brigade's left flank, 1 Dorset were landing well to the east of the beach around WN 36a. Further away from le Hamel and around a slight point in the beach, the Dorsets had a relatively easy landing. While there were mines and a German half platoon position in this area, the enemy had largely relied on the presence of the marsh to deter an Allied landing. According to the Dorsets' post-operational report:

'A Company, on the right, landed at 0725 hours, somewhat east of the correct position and pushed forward to the line of the lateral road, running east from le Hamel, without opposition. ... The company commander Major AAE Jones, Lieutenant Ellis and CSM Howell were all wounded soon after landing by shell and mortar fire. Captain Royle took over command of the company.'

However, the Dorsets' left assault company, B Company, who touched down after a delay at 0737 hours, were not so lucky. They had landed near the enemy half platoon position WN36a and even for the veterans of two previous assault landings, the experience was both unpleasant and costly, as Private Ted Vigour recalled:

'We jumped out under heavy fire and in a great fear and tension. One of our lads fell face down in the water, but nobody stopped. I rushed up the sand and shingle with bullets whizzing past me and actually reached the top of the beach and I heard yells and screams behind me on each side, which sounded bad. Our medics soon attended to the wounded. I lay head down in a state of funk with the remaining lads falling down around me in the same

state, but we grinned in great relief to be alive. The noise was terrific and we heard some Jerry machine-guns going not far away. A lieutenant and sergeant came up and urged us on, so we crawled off that beach a little way and lost two more men. There was green grass and débris and a lot of mist and smoke. When I glanced back, I was amazed at the sight of the invasion fleet. It made me feel we couldn't lose.'

Despite this position, 50th Division was reporting, at 0845 hours, that '... opposition light on left flank of 231 Brigade' and a regimental newsletter published later in June 1944 stated that, as far as the Dorsets were concerned: 'It was NOT until we advanced inland that the really stiff fighting began'. In common with the Americans on OMAHA, 231 Brigade were now to face the field quality troops of 352nd Infantry Division, disposed in depth, rather than the 'elderly gentlemen of the coastal divisions'.

A Sherman Crab of the Westminster Dragoons making its way inland through the scrub behind the beach.

CHAPTER FIVE

LE HAMEL
(Objective DART)
THE COASTAL BATTLE

The fortified coastal village of le Hamel was 231 Brigade's first significant objective. It was thought to be held by two platoons of enemy in le Hamel East (WN37) and le Hamel West (WN38) respectively. In reality the move forward of 352nd Division meant that the village was defended by almost a full company of four platoons of German infantry. 231 Brigade's Intelligence Summary listed the defences:

> ' The defences of le Hamel consisted of three strong points: the first covering the exit onto Jig Green, the second covering the ramp onto the beach at the centre of the sea front and the third covering the exit and beach to the west.
>
> le Hamel EAST: the strong point covering the exit from the beach consists of three MG Pillboxes, also a concrete shelter surmounted by a cupola, sited on top of the ramp, and possibly mounting an anti-tank or infantry gun. A communication trench with open MG emplacements leads to another MG pillbox just to the EAST. All round defence for this position is afforded by a pillbox and several weapon pits with communication trenches sited in gardens on the west side of the road leading from the ramp.'

While the pre-D-Day intelligence report is vague about the presence of an anti-tank gun, 1 Hampshire's post operational report stresses the importance of the Polish 77mm and the fact that this gun did much to deny them vital armoured support. The report goes on to record that, in DART East 'The total strength of the position was about sixty', and that:

> 'The positions were situated in concrete and steel pillboxes in houses fortified with their windows bricked up and in the Hospital which had been fortified and turned into a strong point.'

In the centre of the village's seafront, it was correctly assessed that there were:

> 'Two pillboxes built on the promenade, probably housing one or two MGs and to the rear of which is a concrete personnel shelter, and an open MG emplacement facing SOUTH; also an open emplacement for AA/MG position. Considerable demolition of houses and walls has been carried out... probably to clear the field of fire for landward defences of the strong points.'

To the west, along the promenade, the houses were bricked up for defence or removed and a casemate was built into the sea wall. A 231 Brigade

Intelligence Summary describes the defences of le Hamel west:

'... *consists of two Pillboxes for MGs, one either side of the ramp* [no longer in existence], *and a third on the promenade near the corner of the sea wall – presumably firing inland. A small casemate has been built into the sea-wall and is thought large enough to contain an A tk or infantry gun, which would enfilade the beach to the WEST.*

'*All houses not actually on the promenade in the immediate area have been demolished, and it is therefore thought probable that the houses remaining have been fortified for landward as well as seaward defences.*

'*There are also two or three weapon pits sited to cover the landward side.*'

The majority of this information came from interpretation of vertical and oblique air photographs. With such a long coastline to cover, the Resistance could only help confirm details of the German defences in particular areas to which they had access.

Buildings converted into strongpoints at le Hamel East.

Asnelles church

77mm casemate

The Sanatorium

Chateau Asnelle

Getting off the Beach

With the capture of *Wiederstandnest* 36 by 1 Hampshire, 231 Brigade had secured a small toehold in *Festung Europa*. The destroyers of the naval bombardment group kept the heads of the German defenders down, which enabled the Dorset infantrymen to move westward along the beach to their correct objective of les Roquettes. However, safe in its casemate, the le Hamel 77mm anti-tank gun was keeping the Allied armour, other than a couple of surviving Funnies from Number Two team, well to the east with its destructive fire. Thus, within minutes of the landing, separate armoured and infantry battles were being fought, rather than the closely integrated battle that had been planned.

A Crab from Number Two Team had crossed the beach near 1 Hampshires, between WN36 and le Hamel (WN37), and had began flailing inland. The tank reached the lateral road behind the beach, and, as planned, turned right towards the village strong-points. Within ten minutes of landing, Sergeant Lindsay was in le Hamel unscathed. However, leaving the village to the south-west, he was engaging the Half-

Troop Position at Cabane (WN39), when his solo advance was halted by 88mm guns engaging him from the Puis d'Herode Ridge and knocking him out. Back on the beach, it would appear that, what had been obvious paths beaten by Crabs during rehearsals for D-Day for the infantry and field engineers to follow, were, during actual battle, lost amongst shell holes and sand dunes. However, sappers of 73 Squadron RE were opening a route inland for the infantry, from the beach through WN 36, its barbed wire and surrounding minefields. This was a slow process, completed by hand, that badly held up the Brigade. The dunes around les Roquettes steadily became more congested and the situation was made worse by the arrival of the second flight of infantry LCAs. Landing at 0745 hours, in the

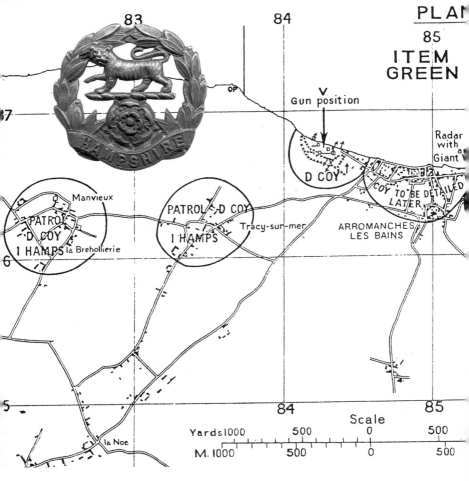

correct place just east of WN36, C Company 1 Dorsets were disconcerted
to find the strong point taken by the Hampshires. Not an A Company 1
Dorset soldier, who should have taken WN 36, was in sight, as they were,
at this stage, still making their way along the beach towards les Roquettes.
Meanwhile, B Company, the other 1 Dorset assault company, had elected
to take a 'short cut' across the Marsh to their objective at the les Roquettes
farm. This route inland took them over an hour-and-a-half to complete, all
the while enduring enemy machine gun and mortar fire from the
Meuvaines Ridge, as well as the sucking mud of the marsh. This explains
why the Germans felt justified in holding the beach in front of the marsh
so lightly.

At 0920 hours, 50th Division's war diary recorded 'Commander 231
Brigade reports everything going to plan but a little late'. Twenty minutes
later an entry records, '1 Hants held up at le Hamel'. 231 Brigade were

80

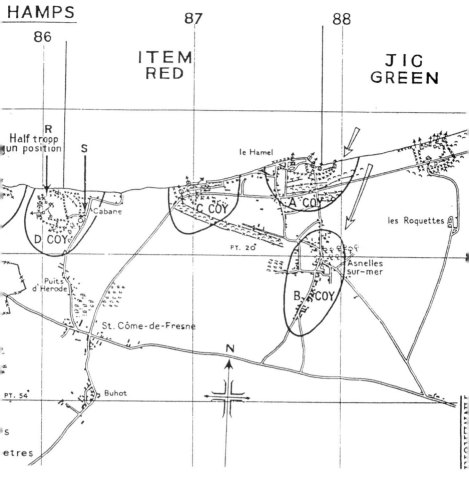

ITEM
RED

JIG
GREEN

R
Half troop
gun position   S

le Hamel

Cabane

C COY

A COY

les Roquettes

D COY

PT. 20

Asnelles
sur-mer

Puits
d'Herode

B COY

St. Côme-de-Fresne

N

PT. 54   Buhot

S

etres

already falling well behind schedule, largely as a result of the 77mm in le Hamel, which prevented the armoured assault teams from creating exits off the beach. Also highly significant was the fact that German regrouping within 352nd Division had brought field-grade grenadiers from other units into 726 Infantry Regiment's positions in le Hamel immediately to the west of JIG. Meanwhile, to the east, on KING beach, 69th Infantry Brigade were making steady progress off their beach against coastal troops and *Ost Truppen*, of 716th Division.

A Company 1 Hampshire had landed nearer to les Roquettes than to le Hamel. Two platoons, as already recorded, attacked the western portion of WN 36, while the remainder of the company headed west along the beach towards le Hamel – directly towards the enemy machine-guns. Urging his men on, 'Company Commander, Major Dick Baines, was killed and the company's other officers were similarly killed or wounded'. Without officers and with most SNCOs similarly out of action, the remains of A Company went to ground in the dunes and ditches. At this stage few Hampshires reached the outskirts of le Hamel.

Back at WN 36, the Royal Engineers eventually produced a single lane off the beach for the infantry. Major Mott led B Company, 1 Hampshire through the gap:

> '... there were notices saying "Achtung Minen" everywhere, I don't think anyone had touched off a mine. The grass was burning and smoke obscured the view. ... We went along the hedge and the whole company was in a long snake with gaps between platoons and it seemed safe unless something opened up in front of us. Soon the smoke cleared enough for me to see Meuvaines Ridge and church, and looking over the hedge, I identified Asnelles spire. Then we came to some ruined and deserted buildings, which were les Roquettes.'

The initial attack on Objective DART.

The farm buildings were the objective of B Company 1 Dorset but they were still, as already recorded, struggling through the Marsh. When they eventually reached les Roquettes, B Company 1 Dorset became the Brigade Reserve with the mission of protecting the beach in case counter-attacks penetrated the forward companies.

Major Mott's B Company mission was to clear le Hamel West, having advanced through A Company 1 Hampshire, who were supposed to have taken le Hamel East. However, finding himself inland and well to the west of his intended position, a new plan was needed. In the absence of their commanding officers, he agreed to work together with Major Nicoll of C Company 1 Dorset, whose company had followed him through the gap at WN 36. Together they planned to advance to the west across the fields drained by ditches that created numerous small fields. They would clear the Dorsets' objectives in Asnelles, and then B Company 1 Hampshire would attack le Hamel East (WN37) from the south. However, having shaken themselves free of the growing chaos between WN 36 and les

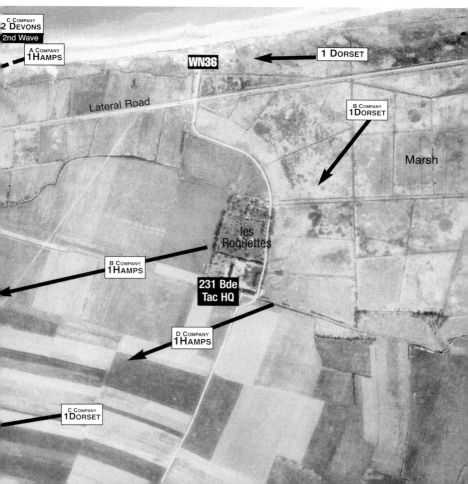

Roquettes, B Company 1 Hampshire were soon held up by enemy fire. Major Mott recalled:

'10 Platoon was giving covering fire from les Roquettes, while 12 followed by 11 went up a hedgerow, ... making for the wall, near which we knew the enemy post was, and indeed, it started to fire at us. The loss of my Company HQ was a blow, as it ruled out wireless communication and I had no runner, so I had to be pretty mobile myself. 12 Platoon came up in savage mood, out for blood, as they had had some casualties. They went in single file up the hedgerow and turned right before anything happened. Then snipers and at least one Spandau opened up on them as they came into view about 150 yards from the wall. Lionel Bawden [Platoon Commander] was hit early on and killed instantly. Sergeant Smith, the platoon Sergeant, a tough man, was also hit and wounded. This left them rather helpless, so I called Graham Elliot to get 11 Platoon on, in any way he could, covering them selves as 10 Platoon's covering fire was by now ineffective. ... at this point, mortar bombs started pitching amongst us, though the troops thought they were mines.

'I went up to 11 Platoon and found a Sherman [flail] near the wall and Graham talking to it and persuading it to have a go at the Bosche, which it did not approve of, as it knew of the anti-tank gun. But it stood and fired shells effectively into the wall and let off a stream of tracer bullets. ... We could see one of the Bosche in a trench system taking shots at us, but the men were slow at answering. They were reluctant to follow Graham, who dashed forward into a crater, and, as no one went with him, I did. We went to near a gap in the corner of the wall, with bullets very close to us from our tank, and crept into the gap.'

An exchange of grenades followed and Major Mott,

'... lay by the wall, feeling very exposed, while Graham went back to the tank and called up some of his men, and Sergeant Bisson also came up with some of 10 Pl. I peered round the wall again and saw no enemy. There was an underground system of trenches and presumably the Bosche thought that they would not last much longer near us.'

Thus, B Company fought their way into Asnelles. Advancing into the main street of the village Major Mott met Major,

'... David Warren and some of Battalion Headquarters. He said that the CO had been wounded and the 2IC killed, and that he had been told to take over command. He wanted me to take a patrol down into le Hamel and see if I could find A Company, of whom there was no news. I collected Graham and several men and we started down the road to le Hamel, some quarter of a mile away. Some of our tanks came down the road towards us. Suddenly I felt a blast and heard a loud crack and splinters came off the road into my face. I didn't know what it was, possibly another mine or stray shell, until I saw that a tank near me had been hit. Then came another blast and another *and it dawned on me that if nothing else there was an anti-tank gun in our way. We turned around and looked for another way into le Hamel.'*

231 Brigade's report on the fighting portrayed an interesting slant on Asnelles's liberation. 'While the battle was raging in Asnelles, the civilian population continued to walk up and down the streets, with little concern as if an exercise was taking place' but at 1015 hours, Brigade Headquarters was reporting that '1 Hants still unable to make any progress in le Hamel'. However, taking a more southerly route, C Company 1 Dorsets and D Company 1 Hampshire made better progress through the southernmost and less strongly defended part of Asnelles.

The German Reaction

The German view of the early stages of the battle on GOLD beach has been summed up by *Oberstleutnant* Fritz Ziegelmann:

'After 0800 hours, the 726 Infantry Regiment reported that, in the section of their right neighbour (an eastern battalion of 716th Infantry Division), the enemy [69 Brigade and 1 Dorset] had landed on a rather wide front, and was advancing with tanks towards Meuvaines. A less strong attack [by 1 Hampshire] – tanks as well – on the east border of Asnelles was repulsed.

'... 352nd Infantry Division saw now clearly that a breakthrough by the enemy armoured troops from Meuvaines to the south made it possible for them to turn to the west without great difficulties, so that at the same time the danger arose of rolling up the divisional front and losing the town of Bayeux.

'352nd Infantry Division required reinforcement for sealing up the

MG34 crew overlook the beach. Many such obsolescent weapons were in use in the Atlantic Wall.

LCTs, armour and men still on the beach, with the obstacles uncleared and now under water, greeted 2 Devon.

> *right flank, which was being torn open; the main task here was to throw the enemy back into the sea from the region around Meuvaines, just as had been frequently practised with the corps reserve (the reinforced 915 Infantry Regiment).'*

However, 915 Infantry Regiment had been marching west towards the American airborne landings at the foot of the Cotentin Peninsular. Oberstleutnant Fritz Ziegelmann continued:

> *'In the course of a telephone conversation with the Corps commander, General of Artillery Marcks, shortly before 0900 hours, I described the situation and requested emphatically the return and subordination of the reinforced 915 Infantry Regiment, since, from the latest reports received, it no longer appeared necessary to send it into the low ground of the Vire south of Carentan. Deployment of the reinforced 915 Infantry Regiment in the region east of Bayeux for the protection of the right divisional flank and a counter-attack towards Crepon – Meuvaines [69 Brigade's area] appeared necessary. The Commanding General agreed to this proposal.'*

However, despite the General's agreement, it took over an hour to contact 915 Infantry Regiment and turn them around. With their French drivers being as unco-operative as they dared and Allied aircraft ranging inland to interdict counter-attack forces, 915 Infantry Regiment was not able to intervene until much later in the day. However, by then it was too late. In the meantime, local German commanders would have to mount their own limited counter attacks. At the operational level, Montgomery's plans to dissipate German operational reserves were working. However, the commander of 1/916 Infantry Regiment, having been largely missed by the bombardment, was confident that he could contain the British between les Roquettes and Asnelles. Even so, the division's scant artillery reserves were allocated to him, as, at the time, the Americans were being held on OMAHA Beach. At this point, it was by no means certain that the landing on JIG Sector would be a success despite the Allied superiority of men and material.

The Second Wave

Leading the second wave were the DD Tanks of B and C Squadrons of the Sherwood Rangers, who had been unable to be 'floated off' to lead the initial assault due to the wind and waves. The eight LCTs had repositioned themselves to run into JIG GREEN EAST at the rear of the first assault serials. At H+35, the Sherwood Rangers, with their screens up, drove off the landing craft about five hundred yards off shore and carried out 'a deep wade, rather than a swim ashore'. The landing was successful with few casualties, as they came ashore well to the east and were out of effective range of the 77mm in le Hamel. However, thirty DD Shermans arriving on the beach produced an instant traffic jam, as they waited for the Royal Engineers to establish beach exits.

Following ten minutes behind the tanks but heading for JIG GREEN WEST, to land behind 1 Hampshire, were 2 Devon. Lieutenant Colonel 'Cosmo' Nevill recalled:

A dead German at WN36. This was the first dead body seen by many of the newer Devon soldiers. Note the dog kennel.

'In our run-in all eyes were glued on the spire of Asnelles church, which made an excellent direction mark. When we got within three hundred yards of the shore, we suddenly realized that the beach obstacles had not been destroyed. We could see quite plainly the unpleasant-looking mines on top of each post. By this time, the tide was so far up that there was no question of grounding below the obstacles. As our speed was reduced to avoid the mines, so we were driven eastwards by a swiftly-flowing tide.'

Private David Powis of the Intelligence Section attached to A Company for landing recalls:

'The landing craft suddenly ground to a halt and down went the ramp. One section of men evacuated the LCA rapidly through the tracer bullets, some of which were now entering the craft as well as passing over the top and presumably to the sides; those men were quickly followed by the second section. ... When Chris and I were able to stand to release the straps holding the folded bicycle to the inside of the LCA, we both jumped up and forward to be sure of getting clear of the landing craft's ramp.

'We hit the water together and went down, and down, and down; would we ever stop this long underwater descent? When our feet eventually touched the bottom of the exceptionally deep channel, we automatically bent our knees and pushed upwards. A brief intake of fresh air refilled our lungs and down we went again. The weight of our equipment should have taken us to the bottom much quicker but the air in our Mae West life belts was impeding our descent. ... A strong sense of relief came when on our next descent we were able to push upwards sooner than before. Again and again we were able to break the surface a little easier for air ... our feet were at last more frequently contacting the sea bed.

'At long last, our heads were at a level where we could get an occasional glimpse of what lay ahead. We had survived that ordeal without discarding a thing [including rifles and the folding bicycle]'

Drowned vehicles and traffic jams on the beach between JIG and KING.

Private Powis recalls seeing 'a couple of professional movie cameras being washed about by the breaking waves', which would account for the lack of film and official pictures of the initial assault on GOLD Beach. He also saw a Sherman that was 'apparently finding it difficult to move forward and turn on the peat strip. It received a direct hit and burst into flames, killing all the crew inside'. Tracer criss-crossing the beach, exploding mortar bombs and smoke from burning tanks and landing craft almost overwhelmed the Devons. Neither training or experience had fully prepared them for their third assault landing.

Lieutenant Colonel Nevill recorded that:

'Then we were ashore directly in front of a German pill-box; the gun had fortunately been knocked out, and a number of German soldiers lay dead beside it. We found that we had landed near les Roquettes.

'We expected to see a nice clear beach complete with all the correct signs neatly arrayed pointing the way to our assembly area. A very different picture greeted us. The beach was covered by a swarm of troops lying flat on their faces, ostrich-like, trying to make as small targets of themselves as possible. All was not well.

'Of the whole battalion, C Company were the only company to land in the right place, and they found that were the first troops to land at that particular spot. Major Bubbles Duke, knowing that his objective was Asnelles, decided to attack the eastern edge of le Hamel, still strongly held by the enemy.'

Thus C Company 2 Devon was committed to the confused fight in le Hamel that was to last all day and cost Major Duke his life. Lieutenant Colonel Nevill continued:

'I had landed in the Dorsets' area. This shook me, as I should have landed in the Hampshires' area. There were no signs of either leading companies, so I turned eastwards along the beach in the hope of finding a gap further along. I met the Brigade Commander who had just landed, and as we were talking I saw some Dorsets move inland through the minefield; I said to the Brigadier: "If I can find any of my chaps, I will bypass Asnelles and go straight for Ryes; – anything to get away from this unhealthy beach".'

According to a Sergeant of a forward section of 200 Field Ambulance, who asked Colonel Nevill if he had seen his unit, he received the dusty reply: 'Field Ambulance be buggered! I can't even find my own bloody battalion'. Eventually finding the scattered elements of 2 Devon, less C Company who were near le Hamel, at approximately 1000 hours:

'The battalion left the beaches in single file, along a narrow footpath the sides of which were supposed to be mined, in the following order; A Coy; followed by advanced battalion HQ; D Coy and B Coy. We suffered casualties from intermittent heavy mortar fire and snipers.'

The Fight for le Hamel

By mid morning four companies of infantry were independently fighting in le Hamel; A and C Company 1 Hampshire were attacking from the east, along with C Company 2 Devon, while B Company 1 Hampshire were probing from the south. Without Hobart's specialist armour or the DD tanks, who were to have led the way ashore, the infantry were making slow progress.

Typical of this phase in the battle is an incident recalled by Corporal Jock Russell, a section commander in 14 Platoon of C Company 2 Devons, who was fighting on the south-eastern outskirts of the village:

'We were held up by a strong-point, which had us nailed down. Every move was stopped by MG fire. Two of my section had already gone down and, although we managed to get within twenty or thirty yards, there was little we could do with small arms. There was a sniper, too. At that point Major Duke ran through the fire and into the ditch that held me and three or four others, and asked what was holding us up. I told him and, holding his binoculars, he immediately crawled out of the ditch to see for himself. I shouted, twice, to him to get down knowing the sniper would be watching but it was too late. A bullet hit him in the head: blood poured out of his mouth: he was killed instantly. C Company lost some good men at le Hamel and the most tragic was Major Duke.'

C Company 2 Devon remained fighting in the western outskirts of le Hamel. However, Major David Warren, who had been summoned to take command of the Hampshires, decided to withdraw A and C Company 1 Hampshire. He could see that an advance down the beach and narrow belt of dunes towards WN37 in the face of concentrated machine gun fire (was not possible). Having amalgamated the two companies into C/A Company, Major Warren directed them to positions on the outskirts of le Hamel East via a route inland of the fire swept beach. Major David Warren recalled C/A Company's move:

'... along the track through les Roquettes towards their objective, but their movement was considerably hampered as all fields in the area for at least one mile inland were wired off, with the well-known "Achtung Minen" notice displayed. On D-Day it was assumed that our intelligence was faulty and that there were many more minefields than had been reported. It was noticed that some mine notices were painted yellow and others white, but it was not until much later that it was discovered that fields with white signs were quite safe and that the yellow signs coincided with known minefields.'

Their route towards le Hamel followed that taken by B Company into Asnelles.

B Company 1 Hampshire had become disorganized in the fighting in Asnelles and reported that 'the enemy position in le Hamel was still very

A Section of 50th Division's infantry moving up to join the D-Day fighting in a village badly damaged by the bombardment.

active'. After a short O Group, Major Warren ordered C/A Company to advance to the line of the road between Asnelles and le Hamel. From here, they were to give covering fire to B Company who would assault the enemy positions centred on the Sanatorium and the bunker on the seafront. C Company 2 Devons, still in the dunes and buildings on the eastern outskirts of the village, made a significant contribution by fixing a proportion of the enemy infantry's attention in the opposite direction to B Company 1 Hampshires' advance.

A few Shermans from the Sherwood Rangers, who had fought free of the traffic jams on the exits from the eastern end of JIG Beach, started to

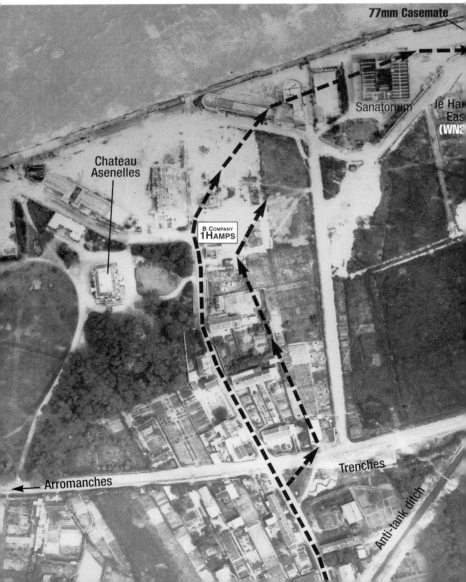

arrive in Asnelles. However, with the landward facing German anti-tank gun still in action they did not last long, as Major Warren recalled:

'... as it arrived at the road junction, there was a terrific explosion and it burst into flames. One member of the crew managed to get out and reported that the gun was loaded and that the flames might fire the shell at any moment. This was most disconcerting as it pointed directly at Battalion Headquarters.'

C/A Company's two hundred yard advance to the road began at 1345 hours and took over an hour to complete, driving back the determined field grade infantry of 352nd Division. The defenders of le Hamel were

AVREs from Assault Team One knocked out by the 77mm gun

Lateral Road

British Armour

proving to be far superior to those coastal troops of 716th Division, who had been holding WN36 and les Roquettes. 'About 12 enemy were taken prisoner during this advance with others being killed or wounded.' Having reached the road, B Company took over the advance. Major Warren continued his account in the post-operational report:

'le Hamel East was still fighting grimly, with most of the opposition coming from the Sanatorium building. B Company closed in on the objective but were held up fifty yards away from the hospital by a torrent of fire. Fortunately at this moment an AVRE appeared coming down the road from Asnelles to le Hamel and was contacted at the road junction. There was no sign of any Flails [all knocked out or leaderless] *or of the troop of Crocodiles which should have landed at H plus 35.*

Major Mott, forward with B Company, recalls the probing attacks mounted on the Sanatorium by 10 Platoon:

'I went back to Sergeant Bisson and told him to make his way forward to the strong point, through the back gardens and trees. Fairly soon he reappeared with about fifteen prisoners ... but there were still shots coming from it. Then David Warren appeared with an AVRE, which fired several shots with its Petard into the concrete.'

Moving up to assist B Company with the evacuation of the wounded, a 1 Hampshire stretcher-bearer recalled an early stage of the final assault on the Sanatorium and WN37:

'Around noon, I was finally creeping up a road, screened by a self-propelled gun. There were many dead Hampshires along the road, so there was no doubting the direction I should take. Many of the casualties had been inflicted by

House to house fighting in the initial stages of the Normandy fighting.

94

enemy in a heavily-fortified Sanatorium, which accounted for several tanks. Its main armament was by now silenced but some of its machine-guns were still active. The SP by which I was crouching opened up at the Sanatorium and nearly deafened me. As I cringed, someone waved at me from the wayside ditch; I stooped to speak just as a line of machine-gun bullets hit the armour where I had been seconds before. In the ditch was one of our stretcher-bearers with a wounded man. Dragging, crawling and crouching we carried the man back to a large captured bunker being used as a dressing station. I was by then too exhausted and scared to go back up the road.'

Major Warren watched as:

'The AVRE closed to within about 50 yards of the Sanatorium and fired one Petard bomb which went off with a great explosion and prompted clouds of dust and smoke. This did not stop the machine gun fire for more than a second or so, so a further round was ordered but it was not until five had been fired that B Company were able to close with the hospital and get into the building.'

The redoubtable Sergeant Bisson led 10 Platoon back into the Sanatorium and led out some thirty shaken Germans, who testified volubly to the effect of the AVRE's Petard, Major Warren summed up his Company's feelings for the German defenders, ' I admired the Bosche who had stayed on resisting to the last with all that bombarding'.

While the main enemy position in le Hamel WN37 had been dealt with

The front of the 77mm casemate showing damage inflicted by 25-pounders of 147 Field Regiment RA firing at close range.

by early afternoon, the casemate on the seafront sheltering the Polish 77mm was still active despite the attentions of tank fire from the east. Company Sergeant Major CSM Bowers recalled:

> 'We crawled through the minefields across a couple of fields, eliminating the Germans that were in the slit trenches there and eventually reached the Sanatorium, at the end of which was the pillbox. I put the men into a firing position and crawled into the Sanatorium and so down onto the top of the pillbox.'

Although Sergeant-Major Bowers does not record it in his account, the AVRE that had effectively ended the enemy opposition in the Sanatorium put one of its forty-pound round into the bunker's rear entrance. At the same time, it is claimed that a Ram self-propelled 25-pounder of 147 (Essex Yeomanry) Regiment RA engaged the front aperture. Whether it was a Royal Artillery or Royal Engineer shell that knocked out the bunker, it was left to Sergeant-Major Bowers to clear it.

> 'The Germans immediately put out a white flag but did not come out. I thought "To hell with you, after all this trouble," and I slipped in a 36 Mills grenade. After the explosion a few seconds passed and out they came shouting "Russkis! Russkis!"'

Oberst Ocker claims not to have had any Russians in 352nd Division but even if these anti-tank gunners were of Russian origin, they fought on well into the afternoon. This is in contrast to the *Ost Truppen* of 441 Battalion on the Meuvaines Ridge, who, according to *Generalmajor* Richter of 716th Division, '... ran away as soon as they could and we could not stop them'.

The German positions in le Hamel East had held out until 1600 hours, through the combined effect of better quality troops and a lack of effective bombardment of their defences. The cost to B Company 1 Hampshire was high, with only about fifty men, out of the original one hundred and twenty who set out from the mother ships ten hours earlier, remaining with Major Mott.

le Hamel West

As early as 0925 hours, 726 Infantry Regiment was reporting 'Three enemy tanks on the eastern wing of WN38 [le Hamel West]; reconnôitring has started'. However, it was not until B Company was clearing the Sanatorium and the bunker containing the Polish 77mm, that C/A Company was sent to clear le Hamel West. 1 Hampshire's post-operational report describes WN38 as:

> '... consisting of a platoon position situated in fortified houses and trenches, well protected with mines and wire ... with fortified houses and at the end of the seawall firing down towards Arromanches [and along the sea front to the east] was an anti-tank gun [50mm]. The strength of the le Hamel West position was thought to be about forty.'

Three destroyers during the morning bombardment had engaged le Hamel. However, according to the Royal Navy's Official History:

> 'No calls for fire were received from the 1st Bn Hampshire Regiment, which was attacking the position, owing to the first and second in command becoming casualties soon after the landing.'

Throughout the morning and early afternoon, unsure of the Hampshires' progress in the village, the destroyers could not shell enemy positions in the village, although they could see that they were still active. However, by late afternoon contact with craft off-shore had been established. Even so, the guns of 25th Destroyer Flotilla could not be used on le Hamel West due to their large 'own troops' danger area but the smaller barrels of the Landing Craft Tank, LCT(Gun) and LCT(Flak) could support C/A Company's attack.

In addition, by mid-afternoon, the surviving vehicles of Hobart's Funnies had cleared the congestion on the beaches, having done as much as they could to create beach exits. Tasked by 231 Brigade to le Hamel, in response to Major Mott's request, a few vehicles were able to join the Hampshires. In a demonstration of their combat effectiveness, an AVRE advanced with the Hampshires, as they systematically cleared the fortified houses in le Hamel West. Without the AVREs to blast their way into the concrete reinforced buildings, the task would probably have been impossible for so few unsupported infantry, who had been in action for twelve hours. Fifty-six years later, Hampshireman Ron Eastman could only find a few a few words to sum up the fighting in le Hamel West:

> 'Bloody awful! After losing so many comrades, I just did what I was told. I didn't expect to survive.'

The defenders of le Hamel West, having been bypassed to the south by 231 Brigade, who were heading for the high ground of Point 54 and Arromanches, could not withdraw and, believing that the Allies would kill prisoners, they fought on. The Germans held their positions in the

View of le Hamel West, along the sea front, with Cabane, the Radar Station and Arromanches in the distance.

buildings until the Hampshires closed in with the AVRE. Meanwhile the LCT(Flak), not having enemy aircraft to engage, poured high volumes of fire into the buildings on the sea front, greatly assisting the infantry. Grenadier Agnussen recorded what it was like to be on the receiving end of the attack:

'The noise was tremendous when the enemy opened fire. I saw two of the strange tanks knocked out. We were firing through what had been large windows which we had boarded and sandbagged, firing our weapons through small holes. We had an excellent and wide field of fire and made a very strong impression on the British who were forced to go to ground and made no way forward against us. Our Feldwebel and Stabsgefreiter were manning machine guns but ... we began to feel that we would not survive as the bombardment continued. More tanks appeared and we began to suffer serious damage to our Wiederstandnest, and several men were killed or injured. It was terrible to hear them moaning and there was no chance of evacuating them. Our Hauptmann was a very strong-willed man and came round continually, exhorting us to hold the enemy until help could reach us. He said the 21st Panzer would relieve us.

The battle seemed to go on and on and soon half our men were casualties and we were running out of ammunition and had nothing to eat at all. Then I received a splinter in my arm and had to lie down while Hans bandaged it up with a paper roll. Then I returned to my position in time to see two British tanks with heavy mortars [Petards] opposite our position. The noise was indescribable as they fired great bombs at us. All hell broke loose as the building began to collapse around us. We were forced to retreat to new positions.'

Clearance of the shell-blasted buildings was a tense and inevitably slow business and it was not until 2000 hours that le Hamel as a whole could be declared clear. Grenadier Agnussen recalled how late in the day:

'I saw the Hauptmann consulting with a Feldwebel, and I guessed they were wanting to surrender, as we had no more ammunition and so many killed and wounded. Our ordeal ended when the Hauptmann waved a small piece of white cloth and Tommy came forward, so we threw out our weapons which were now useless and helped remove the wounded. The bodies of our comrades had to wait.'

Despite the eventual surrender of the defenders in le Hamel West, as 231 Brigade commented, 'Prisoners were still being brought out of the rubble on D+1'.

The battle for le Hamel is an example of the power of the Allied bombardment, in-as-much that it almost totally missed the village's defences during the early stage of the battle, and, consequently, the Germans were able to mount a highly creditable defence. The defenders had not had their senses numbed by the heavy explosions of the

77mm casemate

View from the le Hamel West 50mm anti-tank gun casemate looking east to the 77mm gun.

The le Hamel West position sited to cover the sea wall to the east and the beach to the west.

0mm casemate

Shelters

Six-to eight-feet thick concrete walls protected the le Hamel East 50mm gun from seaward. The sea wall was originally built by the Germans as part of the Atlantic Wall.

bombardment, nor had their morale been undermined. To be fair to the Navy, the casemate containing the Polish 77mm anti-tank gun was cleverly positioned to avoid fire from seaward. For the Allied airforce, the poor weather forced them to use blind bombing techniques and, seeking to avoid cratering the beach, they mistakenly dropped their bombs 3,000 yards inland. On top of all this, the LCTs bearing 147 Field Regiment had, without a Forward Observation Officer (FOO), failed to take part in the 'drenching' of le Hamel with fire. The problem was compounded by the stiffening of the le Hamel defences (WN37 and WN38) with the field-grade infantry from 352nd Infantry Division. From 352nd Infantry Division's perspective, they complained with some legitimacy that their defeat resulted from 716th Infantry Division's failure. Within two hours of the initial landing, their HQ was complaining that '... enemy tanks are attacking Meuvaines and, consequently, the divisional right flank is in danger from our right neighbour's area'.

The weather and sea conditions precluded the landing of DD tanks at H-5, which led to the assault armour fulfilling many of the initial tasks allocated to the two leading squadrons of the Sherwood Rangers. It is also clear that the domination of JIG GREEN by the 77mm anti-tank gun served to separate the infantry from the armour, which was forced to land well to the east. German war diaries report the presence of armour around le Hamel far earlier than the Hampshires did. However, few of the leading tank crews survived to report their activities. 'Co-operation' between armour, infantry and the supporting arms had broken down, and, fighting on their own, many isolated tanks were knocked out in the initial stages of the battle.

CHAPTER SIX

FIGHTING INLAND

While 1 Hampshire and C Company 2 Devon were fighting in le Hamel, the remainder of 231 Brigade Group were forcing their way inland. However, with the delay in opening beach exits and the separation of the infantry from the armour, despite Brigadier Stanier's initial optimism that 'things were going to plan', the battle developed quite differently.

1 Dorset's Advance to Point 54

The advance inland from les Roquettes, as has already been covered, was spearheaded by companies of Hampshiremen and Dorsets, who were attempting to execute their original orders. 1 Dorset's main objectives, however, lay on the ridge of high ground that extended south from the town of Arromanches to the village of Ryes. The pre-D-Day assessment of the main enemy position on the ridge at Puits d'Herode was that it was a strong point with,

> 'An infantry platoon position centred on an Arty OP, which probably connects with the artillery troop position ... [a thousand yards to the south-west]. The position is surrounded by a broad belt of wire sited approximately 100 yards from the trenches.

> 'There are three small trench systems centring on a large hut. It is thought that Arromanches cannot been seen from this position, although it is on the high ground, and that the main task is to protect the OP from the NE and East.'

However, as elsewhere, the arrival of infantry from 352nd Division had been largely missed by Allied intelligence and the ridge was, in fact, held far more strongly than had been expected. What had been thought to be a single platoon position was found to be a network of mutually supporting positions in company strength.

To reach the foot of the ridge, 1 Dorset had to cross open country that 'if all had not gone well with 69 Brigade's attack', would have been dominated by enemy positions, in 716th Division's area, on the Meuvaines ridge. In addition, positions of unknown strength lay in the southern part of Asnelles. In what proved to be an optimistic assessment, the 231 Brigade Intelligence summary thought that the village was 'occupied only by the headquarters of the company holding the sea front at le Hamel'. However, the 14 May edition of the intelligence map, which was issued to the assault troops, clearly shows trenches, bunkers and machine guns on the eastern outskirts of Asnelles.

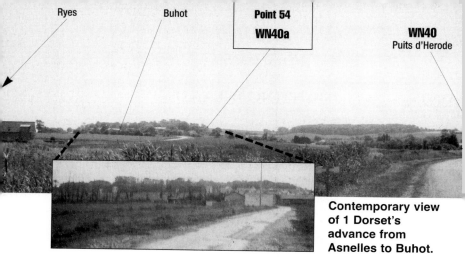

Ryes   Buhot   Point 54 WN40a   WN40 Puits d'Herode

Contemporary view of 1 Dorset's advance from Asnelles to Buhot.

As has already been recorded, leaving les Roquettes at 0915 hours, C Company 1 Dorsets became embroiled in fighting in the southern end of Asnelles. Rather than the expected enemy company headquarters, the Germans were in at least platoon strength and used the cover afforded by the sturdy buildings to good effect. Major Nicoll and his company, to the left of the Hampshires, approached the southern end of the long, thin village and, according to the Dorsets' war diary:

> '... encountered heavy MG fire from the southernmost houses. 15 Pl (Lt Hamilton) were eventually held up and Major Nicoll put in 13 Pl (Lt Widenbank) further south, who dealt with the position, killing 6 and capturing 10 Germans.'

This short paragraph covers two hours' shooting, movement and infantry fighting amongst the honey-coloured stone buildings of southern Asnelles. It should be noted, at this stage, 14 Platoon was still missing, having been separated from the remainder of C Company on landing. A recent arrival in 15 Platoon 1 Dorset, Londoner Joe Roland recalled that:

> 'The Germans were good soldiers and knew what they were doing and our task was difficult because our mortars and guns [artillery] were not yet ashore. We had what we called a firefight, to cover our other platoons into the village, further to the left. Once they were in, the enemy stopped firing back at us and we were able to advance to the village. When we were in, the Jerries started to surrender as we came in behind them.'

Corporal Carter, also of 15 Platoon, according to his Military Medal citation:

> '... although wounded, he refused treatment, insisting on taking part in the assault on Asnelles, where he led his section with great determination and vigour, [during the fighting in Asnelles]. The platoon comd and platoon sergeant both became casualties, and he took command of the platoon...'

The Dorsets' war diary records that at '1130, C and D Coys continue

CHURCH

WN39
Half-Troop Gun
Position Cabane
Command
Post Casemates

advance towards Buhot' and the Battalion's next objective, Point 54 (WN40a). The Battalion Second in Command, Major Bredin, wrote:

> 'Both companies then continued to advance across very open country. ...
> A good deal of fire was brought to bear on the two companies and there was
> a steady stream of casualties'.

As was so often the case, many of the casualties were junior commanders. The Dorset's, under fire all the way, reached the small village of Buhot (known to the Dorsets as 'Boohoo') at 1330hours. Buhot lay at the foot of Point 54.

C Company, on the right, crossing the road from St Come-de-Fresne to Ryes, pressed on up-hill. 15 Platoon, who were again leading, were promptly driven back by an unexpectedly strong enemy position in the copse at Point 54. Lieutenant Hamilton was wounded. They took cover in the hedgerow at the foot of the hill and Corporal Carter resumed command, organized his platoon and gave covering fire to 13 Platoon. Corporal Sam Thompson, who had already earned a Military Medal in Italy, spearheaded 13 Platoon's fight up a track to Point 54, using fire and manoeuvre. He and a rifleman from his section, working as a pair, determinedly pushed on up-hill into enemy fire using the flanking ditch and hedgerow as cover. This was an occasion when just two men, commanded by an extremely brave and highly competent junior NCO, led a successful battalion advance. For this action and others later in the day, Corporal Thompson earned a well-deserved Distinguished Conduct Medal. Having broken into the position at the top of the track, the remainder of 13 Platoon cleared the enemy trench system. At 1400 hours, the battalion watchkeeper was recording that:

> 'C Coy in possession of Pt 54, after stiffer opposition than anticipated.
> seven Germans were killed and two officers and fifteen ORs were made
> prisoner. C Coy took up positions to support D Coy's attack on Puis
> D'Herode. D Coy pushing south through Buhot surprised and captured a
> coy of German pioneers with their transport.'

Questioning of the prisoners taken on Point 54 (WN 40a) quickly

Asnelles

Buhot

15 Platoon

Outflanking route taken by Corporal
Thompson and 13 Platoon

Lieutenant X
Hamilton
wounded

POINT 54 **WN 40a**

C Company tried to advance across this field but were checked by
fire from a platoon position on Point 54.

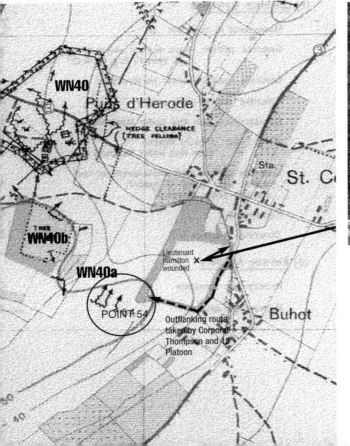

WN40

Puits d'Herode

HEDGE CLEARANCE
(TREE FELLING)

Sta.

St. C

WN40b

Lieutenant
Hamilton X
wounded

WN40a

POINT 54

Outflanking route
taken by Corporal
Thompson and 13
Platoon

Buhot

The covered track
from Buhot to Point
54 up which Corpor
Thompson DCM, M
led his section in a
assault on the
unexpectedly stron
German position. In
the wood at the top
of the track Germa
trenches are still to
be seen today.

A platoon commander from 1 Dorset searches for the enemy in close country covered by members of his HQ.

On 50th Division's left flank, 69 Infantry Brigade made swift progress inland against relatively weak opposition.

established that these were not coastal troops of 726 Regiment but Grenadiers of 1/916 Infantry Regiment. However, it is thought that the pioneers captured by D Company were from 726 Regiment, who had been brought forward to act as infantry in a counter attack role with 1/916.

2 Devon, the Grande Riviere and Ryes

Lieutenant Colonel Nevill wrote that following the Dorsets and Hampshires towards les Roquettes,

> 'The battalion left the beaches in single file, along a narrow footpath the sides of which were supposed to be mined, in the following order: A Coy; followed by advanced battalion HQ; D Coy and B Coy.'

While the Dorsets' main objectives lay on the Point 54/Puits d'Herode ridge to the west, 2 Devon's initial objective was the village of Ryes, which lay at the southern end of the ridge some three miles inland. Lieutenant Colonel Nevill's original plan was to assemble his battalion in Asnelles before pushing south down the line of la Grande Riviere. However, the delay in taking Asnelles forced him to take a more direct and more exposed route.

However, before advancing south, the Devons, 'in some disarray', had to fight off German counter-attacks.

A and B Companies brushed aside enemy in the area of les Roquettes and then once they reached the line of the new coast road they experienced more determined counter-attacks. A series of entries in 352nd Division's War diary illustrates the Germans' attempts to contain 231 Brigade:

'0825. Report from 352nd Artillery Regiment: 3rd Battalion/352nd Artillery Regiment reports: Of the tanks landed near defence work No 35, several (about six) have been put on fire or made immobile by anti-tank and land defence guns.

'0831. Chief of Staff 726th Grenadier Regiment: 2nd and 1st Battalions/916th Grenadier Regiment have to prepare for an attack to the right in the direction to Meuvaines. Readiness to be reported.

'0835. Commanding General reports: Situation on the right wing near Meuvaines and Asnelles is difficult; Meuvaines is in enemy hands. Ahead of Asnelles, our anti-aircraft guns have shot six tanks. Gen Kraiss proposes to launch an attack by Kampfgruppe Meyer (minus one battalion), reinforced by the bulk of 352nd Panzerjager [assault-gun] battalion, in order to throw back to the coast and into the sea the enemy infantry and tanks penetrating our right wing.

'0905. WN 37 [le Hamel East] asks for reinforcements. Enemy infantry and tanks heading to Meuvaines.'

This latter entry referred to the more southerly route that 2 Devon were being forced to take by the situation in Asnelles. With German reserves having been prematurely tasked to the west of the divisional area, the local counter-attacks by 916th Regiment lacked punch and immediate effect as this signal log entry records: '1000 hours. From 352nd Div to Kampfgruppe Meyer: When are you going to start? In what direction?'

Despite the slowness of 916th Regiment's start, the Germans managed to impose significant delays on the Devons. The Battalion diarist recorded that,

'During all this time communications with Coys had been scanty and the Commanding Officer had great difficulty in getting his orders for a change of plan to the Coys concerned'.

Private Powis was one of those who was working to find information and pass messages:

Lieutenant Colonel 'Cosmo' Nevill.

'*Enemy machine guns were now firing along the road from our right-hand side when we reached it, so we quickly returned fire that way as well as to the front, where we could see the Germans running towards us. Our numerically decreased company entered the field to our front to take over from us and get to grips with the Germans in hand-to-hand fighting. ... We were able to see that they were engaged in close combat with grenades, small arms, and bayonets I cannot be sure how far we went up the road inland before stopping for the IO to discuss the situation with the battalion CO, who had moved up to the rear of B Company. This company was diminishing in numbers and we had to be constantly ready for the possibility of a German breakthrough. The CO explained that he knew A Company were engaging the enemy too far to the right, thus opening a gap between them and B Company.*

The IO told me to take the bicycle, and go back to the [Old] *Coast Road and turn left to where A Company was believed to be. I was to find the Company Commander and tell him to disengage and move back to the left.*'

Riding back down the road, Private Powis was the target of German machine gunners. However, being a furiously peddling target, flitting out of sight between clumps of remaining hedgerow, he eluded them. Powis continued:

'*I was forced to dismount and lift the bicycle over a large mound of lifeless German bodies, strewn across the road. ... One German still had a hand grenade clasped tightly in his right hand, obviously about to throw it when he was riddled with bullets in the chest and had fallen on his back. Another was lying on his back minus his steel helmet and lay in the shallow dry ditch bordering the road, he was handsome blue-eyed blond and must have been over six feet tall. The back of his head was missing and the space had been filled with straw, lots of which lay loosely around that spot.*

'*It must have been somewhere about two hundred yards along the road ... that I found myself amongst familiar Malta veterans of A Company. None of them could tell me where their Company Commander might be but they took me to their platoon officer... The officer carefully copied all my entries onto his own map, thanked me for the information and said that he was going forward and would pass on the details. Before my departure he explained to me that one reason A Company had been forced to move to the right was because they had learned that 1st Hampshire had been badly cut up and lost a lot of men, including most of their senior ranks.*

'*Through the hedges, on the way back, I spotted German infantry moving rapidly towards the coast road and had to get down to avoid being seen by them. There were men of my Battalion moving inland to the left. I informed those nearest me about the advancing Germans but they were fully engaged with the Germans to the front of them.*'

Without support, these initial counter-attacks by Meyer's 1/916 Grenadier

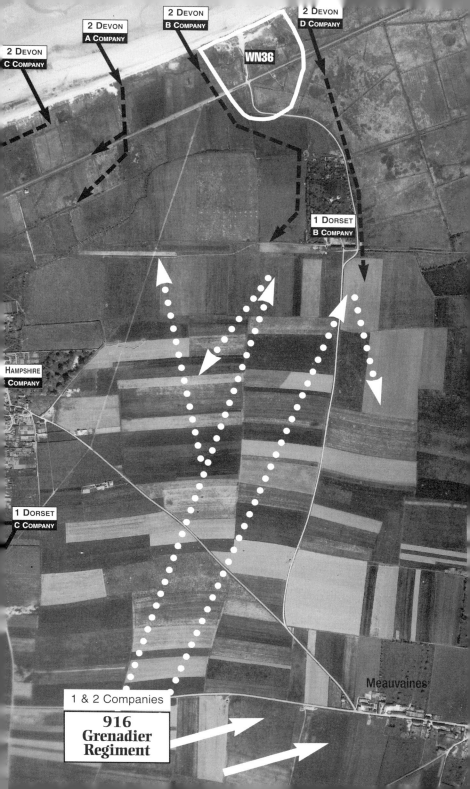

2 DEVON
C COMPANY

2 DEVON
A COMPANY

2 DEVON
B COMPANY

2 DEVON
D COMPANY

WN36

1 DORSET
B COMPANY

HAMPSHIRE
COMPANY

1 DORSET
C COMPANY

1 & 2 Companies

916
Grenadier
Regiment

Meauvaines

Regiment were beaten off by the Devons with small arms fire, skilfully controlled by veteran section commanders. In the open fields, the Germans suffered heavy casualties. Another counter-attack would have to await the arrival of the LXXXIV Corps' force based on 915 Infantry Regiment. With the confusion at WN 36 and les Roquettes, it is perhaps fortunate that the Germans were not able to launch this counter-attack before 0900 hours, as it would have stood a far greater chance of throwing 231 Brigade back into the sea.

Counter-attack defeated, the Devons advanced inland. Lieutenant Holdsworth was, however, having problems with his map.

'I remember that one of the physical features which would help me to find the correct way inland was la Grande Riviere. But there was no sign of anything that looked remotely like a Grande Riviere. However, in chivvying my lot to get on, serious contemplation of the whereabouts of what sounded like a fairly big river was not possible.

'In a ditch in a small copse ahead of me, I saw my CO bending over my Company Commander who had been hit rather badly. As he waved me on, my CO moved his right foot. Where it had been was now a puddle of dirty brown water. He was standing in the middle of la Grande Riviere!'

Lieutenant Colonel Nevill went on to explain that:

'After assembling in the valley just south of Asnelles village the advance continued, and we began to think that we were through the enemy crust and we should have little difficulty in seizing Ryes. We were wrong. When A Coy reached a point about 1000 yards north of Ryes they came under intense Spandau fire, at close range, from enemy hidden in thick hedges. This became close fighting with a vengeance.'

Private Keenor was with A Company and, as his MM Citation describes, he

'... was manning a Bren gun in the leading platoon. When this platoon was held up by enemy LMG fire, a patrol tried to work forward up a covered ditch. They came under fire from a Spandau, which was trained on the ditch, and would undoubtedly have suffered severe casualties had not Pte Keenor leapt out of the ditch into the open and engaged the Spandau with his Bren. He remained in this position for several minutes while magazines were thrown to him across the ditch. His prompt action and deadly fire allowed the remainder of the patrol to move to a flank and destroy the enemy.'

This enemy position was in fact 'a triple series of outposts, which had to be dealt with one by one'. The Battalion war diary records that there were other difficulties:

'The country here was extremely close and it was impossible to locate the enemy MGs & snipers as they held their fire to short ranges. In trying to adv in face of this opposition, A & D Coys suffered many casualties.'

The German view of the situation that General Kraiss had to control is best

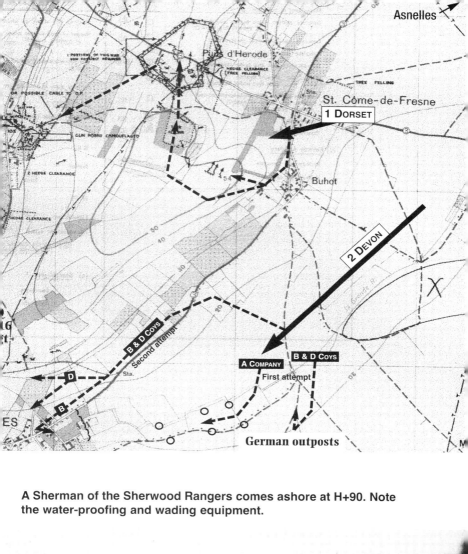

Asnelles

Puis d'Herode

St. Côme-de-Fresne

1 Dorset

Buhot

2 Devon

B & D Coys
Second attempt

B & D Coys

A Company

First attempt

D

B

ES

German outposts

A Sherman of the Sherwood Rangers comes ashore at H+90. Note the water-proofing and wading equipment.

summarized by selected entries from his Headquarters signal log.

'1317. Reports from the right neighbouring 716th Infantry Division: Artillery reports forty tanks of the heaviest type heading towards Ryes [the arrival of the Sherwood Ranger's Shermans and SP artillery].

'1405. Reports from 726 Grenadier Regiment: The attack of 1st Battalion/916 Grenadier Regiment on Meuvaines had to be turned to the direction of St Come, as eight tanks with mounted infantry were attacking defence works 40a, 40b and 40c [this was 1 Dorset and C Squadron Sherwood Rangers' attack on Puits d'Herode].

'1434. Near Ryes, forty tanks are said to be moving south-west.'

The number of Sherwood Rangers' tanks was exaggerated in these reports but it is clear that 2 Devon's advance had deflected another German counter-attack from 69 Brigade's area to Ryes. Lieutenant Colonel Nevill continued his account of his attack on Ryes:

'Every means was tried to dislodge the enemy from the trees and hedges. We had no artillery or mortar support as they had not yet landed [not established communications]. *The only fire support we had was from our destroyer and our Forward Observer Bombardment, Captain Dupont* [though wounded], *brought accurate fire to bear on the outskirts of Ryes. Under cover of this fire, Major Frank Saddler tried to push on and B and D Coys tried to turn the flanks but were held up when crossing the open country. Lieutenant Foy and a portion of his platoon were taken prisoner in the mêlée that ensued.'*

Having been checked in his advance by 1/916 Grenadiers, whose HQ had been in dugouts to the north-west of Ryes, Lieutenant Colonel Nevill, now reinforced by M10s of 102 Anti-Tank Regiment, changed his plan. He left A Company astride the 'river', to engage and fix the enemy in place. Moving B and D Companies 500 yards right, to the line of the road into Ryes, he bypassed the enemy in the hedges east of the village and broke into Ryes. The next entry in 2 Devon's war diary records that at,

'1625, B Coy reached Ryes and occupied it with only slight opposition.

1630, The CO with 2 sections of D Coy pushed on to high ground N. West of Ryes, which was found to be unoccupied. Later C Coy and the remainder of D Coy moved up to this area.

1630, A Coy reported a counter-attack, which they held.'

The attack had taken the Devons into the area of 1/916's Headquarter dugouts at the foot of the ridge, which had been hastily abandoned. Back in Ryes, Lieutenant Holdsworth described his platoon's entry into a part of the village:

'My platoon followed me there. I supposed we "captured" it, but only in the sense that we occupied it now instead of the Germans who, presumably, had withdrawn, leaving only a sniper. He shot my Platoon runner in the head and then disappeared.

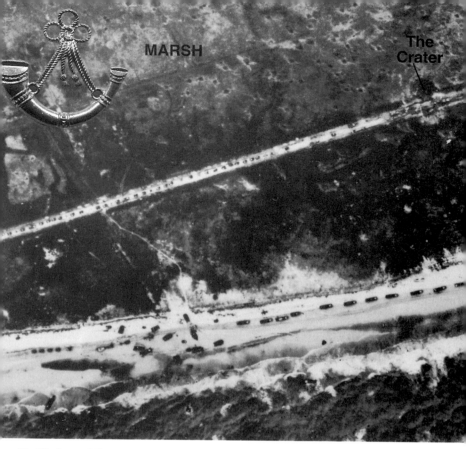

MARSH

The Crater

Traffic jam at the crater on the lateral road. Late morning on D-Day. Note the number of bomb and shell craters in the marsh. Inset: The Sherwood Rangers cap badge.

'This kept us on edge for a bit and we searched the village very carefully indeed before satisfying ourselves that there were no other Germans about. Indeed, there weren't any French people either. But plenty of dead cows.

'Communication with other platoons was non-existent. ... But somehow the other two platoon commanders in my company collected their troops together and we all joined up in more or less the place we should have been. It was by then well into the afternoon.'

At 1638 hours, 352nd Division recorded, 'Report from 726th Grenadier Regiment: Ryes is in enemy hands'. The Devons put Ryes into a state of defence and dispatched platoons to clear the scrubby slopes of the ridge towards Point 54. However, according to PWs that the Devons questioned, and this is something that 352nd Division's war diary confirmed, HQ 1/916 Grenadier Regiment had abandoned its positions, to lead the

113

counter-attack towards Meuvaines. Some of the prisoners revealed that they were from a weak company formed by the Divisional NCO School. They reported that they had been brought up to support a counter-attack by 1/916 Regiment and were advancing north-east through Ryes and its orchards, when they encountered the leading elements of the Devons coming from the opposite direction.

Armour

While the infantry were fighting their way inland, the main concentration of armour and self-propelled guns was struggling to get clear of the beach and through the gaps that the engineers were clearing. Fire from the le Hamel casemate had forced the LSTs to land their tanks on the eastern portion of JIG GREEN near WN 36a. From this area it was relatively easy to reach the Lateral Road behind the beach, but getting tanks across the four hundred yards of marsh that lay beyond was impossible. Therefore, to join the infantry that they were meant to support, the tanks had to follow the lateral road westward. On this single route, the majority of Brigade Group's 200+ armoured vehicles became ensnared in a traffic jam. A large crater, easily visible on the air photograph on the previous page, was one of the causes of the delays. Trooper Joe Minogue was in the first Crab tank to encounter the hole:

> *'Further along the road we were trying to negotiate a bomb crater right in the centre of the road and suddenly the tank began to slide into the crater. We obviously couldn't move and so we got out and by this time the infantry [1 Dorset] had got off the beach. Their officers were most impatient about the fact that we were holding up their advance and they cursed and swore in those fancy voices that ordinary soldiers learned to imitate so well, things like, "I say, old chaps, can't you move that damn thing out of the way?"*

One of the well camouflaged anti-tank guns on Point 22 that engaged British armour leaving JIG Beach.

Left: Former Soviet Army PoWs who 'volunteered' to serve in the Wehrmacht abandoned dominating positions on the Meuvaines Ridge.

Eventually another tank came along and gave us a tow out of this hole.'

Once a route was established from the beach, through the minefields and the marsh, the armour's problems was far from over. The next difficulty was the anti-tank guns positioned on the high ground to the east and west. A late morning entry in 50th Divisions war diary recorded:

'HQ 8 Armd Bde Gp state that "opposition on the beaches was only slight except for two 88mm guns on the high ground Pt 22, which brewed up four Notts Yeo tanks on the beach." These guns were 1000 yards from the nearest point of the beach, and had a good command of the assault area. 90 Fd Regt RA also recorded the presence of these guns. At 0900 hrs "two 88mm guns were in action and at 1030 hrs, two signallers of an OP party were killed by these guns which also caused many infantry casualties."'

It is thought that the crews abandoned their guns on Point 22 when they found that they had been deserted by the *Ost Truppen* infantry who were supposed to be holding positions around them. On the western flank, the defenders of the Point 54 area recorded that 'the anti-aircraft gun in WN40 [Puits d'Herode] has shot three or four tanks'. The advancing infantry eventually cleared these dangerous interlocking arcs of anti-tank fire and the armour could move inland.

Puits d'Herode

As already explained, through their own unsupported efforts, 1 Dorset had secured a toe-hold on the ridge above Buhot at Point 54. At 1400 hours, Lieutenant Colonel Norie, with his Tac HQ, arrived from the beach and joined C and D Companies. Climbing the ridge to Point 54 and moving

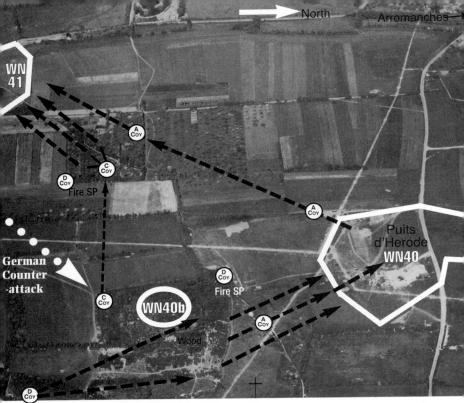

1 Dorset's attack on Puits d'Herode (WN40) and the 'Arromanches One' Battery (WN41).

through the copse to its forward edge, the CO, made his plan. C Company, who had reorganized on Point 54, were to remain in position and provide fire support to D Company who would climb the ridge to the south, and clear a defended wood (WN40b), before attacking the main Puits d'Herode position. D Company found the wood more strongly defended than had been expected. 18 Platoon were leading and, while moving through open country, both platoon commander and sergeant became casualties. The advance came to a halt. However, Corporal Hawkins took command and reaching the wood line:

The view from Point 54 West to the wood and Puits d'Herode. It was from here that fire support was provided by infantry and C Squadron's Shermans.

> *'Went forward on a personal recce, located the enemy post and returned to his platoon. With great skill he then led his men round the enemy's flank, delivered a sharp attack and destroyed all enemy resistance'.*

Corporal Hawkins was awarded a Military Medal. The Battalion's report records that 'after some fierce fighting, 18 Platoon managed to capture an 81mm mortar detachment, a *Spandau* post and an anti-tank gun'. Reaching the northern edge of the wood, the remainder of the company was unable to cross the hundred yards of open ground, swept by machine gun fire, to the perimeter wire of the Puits d'Herode position.

At this point Lieutenant Colonel Norie realized that a properly co-ordinated, deliberate attack was required. Fortunately, C Squadron, Sherwood Rangers had joined A Company in Buhot at the foot of the ridge and artillery fire support was now available from 90 Field Regiment. It had taken a considerable time for the self-propelled guns to shake free of the traffic and find sufficient space to deploy the batteries. The plan was simple: D Company were to remain in position on the northern edge of the wood and give fire support; C Company was moved to the south-west corner of the wood to provide flank protection and additional fire support; while C Squadron's Shermans, firing over the infantry from Point 54, were to add HE and machine-gun fire. Superimposed on all this was an artillery fire plan, fired by 90 Field Regiment. Meanwhile, A Company was brought up from reserve to deliver the assault from the wood.

With the support of both tanks and artillery, Captain Royle led his company forward, as the very close fire plan lifted from Puits d'Herode onto German depth positions to the west. Following the bombardment, the two concertina wire fences and minefield presented few problems but Bangalore Torpedoes (two and a half inch pipes packed with explosive) were pushed under the wire and detonated to provide additional assault routes. There were no casualties from mines, as the infantry were able to use the shallow overlapping shell holes as a route across the seventy-yard-wide minefield. In the position, the German infantry were stunned by the weight of fire, but one group of enemy fought on and,

> *'Sergt Terry distinguished himself by overcoming personally the resistance of the locality, and receiving the surrender of a large portion of the enemy'.*

When the killing in the huts and three trench systems stopped, A Company took forty prisoners. The handful of German artillerymen captured amongst the infantry were from an observation post for the artillery battery just to the west (WN41).

WN40
Puits d'Herode

Company

Arromanches

During the attack on Puits d'Herode, C Company was on the Battalion's open left flank and, while A Company's assault was going in, they were counter-attacked from the west by enemy in approximately platoon strength. These Germans were also from the WN41 position six hundred yards to the west of the wood. The Company Second-in-Command, Captain RW Tucker, was dispatched with the remains of 13 Platoon to deal with this new threat. Corporal Sam Thompson was again instrumental in overcoming the enemy. His DCM citation states that he,

'... *immediately moved his section to deal with it* [the enemy] *and killed, wounded or captured all of them'*.

To complete their D-Day missions in their entirety, 1 Dorset had to clear 352 Artillery Regiment's battery position a thousand yards to the west of Puis d'Herode. The battery was sited to cover le Hamel and Jig Beach. 231 Brigade's Intelligence Summary described the WN41 position:

'*There are four gun emplacements, well camouflaged, two of them possibly under huts, and two hidden in an orchard. The position is thought to be occupied by a troop of 105mm gun howitzers. The position is protected by thick wire on its eastward side. There are eight weapon pits covering the wire and connected by a trench system.'*

Also nearby were ammunition bunkers and what was either an abandoned, dummy or alternative gun position. In all, it was a large objective that would take more than one company to attack.

The German battery commander's day had started with the battery being shelled by HMS *Emerald's* seven six-inch guns, which limited the effectiveness of the battery's engagements around le Hamel.

Impressed by the effect on the enemy of the fire support given to A Company's attack, Colonel Norie decided to repeat the formula again. D Company was to combine with 90 Field Regiment to provide fire support from the area of the copse to the south-west. A and C Companies were to deliver the assault with tanks of the Sherwood Rangers in intimate support. The fire plan began as scheduled and the Dorsets advanced alongside the Shermans. The tanks led the way through the wire, halted and deluged the enemy positions with HE and machine-gun fire as the infantry closed in. However, the Germans had gone, leaving behind the guns and seemingly all their equipment.

In a debrief, the Artillery Commander of 352nd Division explained that most of his twenty-four guns that could fire on JIG Beach did so until they had fired their first line scale of three hundred and fifty rounds. In most cases, they ran out of ammunition at around 1600 hours, which is the time that 1 Dorset was preparing to attack, and when,

118

Lieutenant Colonel Norie DSO

across the Brigade, the tempo of operations increased. The German batteries were intended to be re-supplied by truck but with the skies above the battlefield dotted with the ever-present Allied fighter-bombers, no ammunition reached the batteries and, without transport, the guns had to be abandoned.

B Company 1 Dorset, who had been left behind at les Roquettes, after their adventure in the marsh, as Brigade Reserve, moved to Ryes. However, with 56 Brigade heading inland to Bayeux, 231 Brigade was in effect the reserve, even though the Hampshires were still fighting along the coast line. B Company 1 Dorset arrived in Ryes to find that 2 Devon intended to halt in the village for the night, before completing their tasks the following morning. The remainder of the Dorsets took up positions on the ridge between Puits d'Herode and Ryes. Finally, after a day's very hard fighting in the eastern outskirts of le Hamel, C Company 2 Devon also rejoined its battalion.

A camouflaged self-propelled gun in the open area inland of les Roquettes. Artillery support greatly speeded up operations in the afternoon of D-Day.

Afternoon on D-Day: troops of 56 Infantry Brigade cross JIG Beach after their delayed landing.

The only US troops to land on GOLD come ashore. Their heavy 155mm guns were under command of 50th Division on D-Day.

CHAPTER SEVEN

ARROMANCHES

Out of season, Arromanches is a quiet seaside town, nestling in a valley that runs down to the sea from the surrounding hills: much the same as before war brought it fame. However, the damage suffered by Arromanches was caused, not so much by the fighting, but by the Allied use of the town in the days, weeks and months after D-Day. Having fought westwards along the coast from JIG Beach, Arromanches was planned to be 1 Hampshire's last major D-Day objective.

The Hampshires' progress westward, against better quality enemy troops than had been anticipated, was slow. However, while Major Warren and two companies were fighting in le Hamel, enemy positions barring the way to Arromanches were attacked by other elements of 1 Hampshire.

The Cabane 'Half Troop Position' – WN39
An early edition of 231 Brigade's Intelligence Summary describes the 'Half Troop Position' sited on a hillside, 'overlooking the Cabane area to the east':

'This position is surrounded by a double belt of wire, which may contain mines. It consists of two open emplacements for light infantry guns, probably 75mm. These might be either French pattern (range 12,800 yds) or of the German infantry gun pattern (range 3,800 yds), and are sited to fire east along the beaches [they in fact proved to be of Russian origin].

There are three concrete shelters connected with the emplacements by a trench system, and three weapon pits sited to cover the defensive wire. Forward of the emplacements, a small communications trench leads to what is thought to be a pillbox.

A casemate is now nearly completed at 861864, and as the [field]

Cabane Church

Casemates WN39

A not-very-accurate mosaic of oblique air photographs showing coastline from Cabane to Arromanches. This was carried on D-Day by Major Bredin (1 Dorset).

emplacement behind appears to be unoccupied, this gun may now be sited in the casemate. It must not be overlooked, however, that a third gun may be added.'

Little more than a month later, the Hampshires faced further pillboxes and a second gun in a completed casemate, with a third under construction but without a gun. Rommel and the Todt Organization worked day and night to thicken up *Festung Europa*, as the Allied invasion approached. Initial D-Day plans and briefings needed frequent updating, as air recce reports from the Normandy coast came in during May 1944.

The plan was for the battery to be engaged by the three 5.9-inch guns of Lieutenant Commander Koudys's Dutch gunboat, HMNS *Flores*. Sited so

The post-war road to Arromanches cuts through what was once the centre of this defensive system. This casemate received a direct hit, but the gun survived and was able to carry on firing.

Arromanches

that the cliffs gave it protection from seaward, WN39 needed the gunboat, with its shallow draft, to get close inshore and engage the battery from the east. D Company, who were to be 1 Hampshire's reserve in earlier phases, was to attack the battery.

In the event, while B and A/C Company were still involved in the protracted fighting in le Hamel, D Company, commanded by Major Littlejohns, by-passed the fighting by taking a southerly route through Asnelles. The Company crossed some low ground and approached the enemy position from the south-east. By early afternoon, at about the same time that the Dorsets received tank support, five of the remaining tanks from B Squadron, Sherwood Rangers, provided welcome support to D Company. Their firepower helped the Hampshiremen overcome the flanking fire from Puis d'Herode, which covered the approaches to the 'Half Troop Position'. Private Sam Curton recalls that:

> 'We had been under fire all the way from the beach but as we got close to the ridge we could see the battery behind the church. There was plenty of chalky white soil, so it wasn't difficult to spot. This was the first time, since the beach, that I felt that I was the Jerry's personal target. Major Littlejohns led us on a route that avoided the fire from the guns but the Spandaus were bad enough. The tanks moved ahead and around us shooting up the battery. When we got in the wire, the Jerries were quick to surrender: most were pretty bomb-happy and a sorry sight.'

During the fighting at Cabane, Major Littlejohns won the Military Cross. An extract from his citation reads:

> '... without hesitation he organized his coy for an attack on an arty battery dominating the whole beach area. Despite very heavy shell and MG fire, Major Littlejohns led his coy forward. The fire increased in intensity, and the coy was held up. Major Littlejohns once more took the coy forward, and finally succeeded in capturing the position. The success of this attack

Poits d'Herode
WN40

WN39

Shelter complex and the Battery Command Post (CP) at the Half-Troop position

Entrance to the CP.

A Tobruk machine gun position on top of one of the shelter bunkers makes an excellent garden terrace.

This casemate housed a captured Russian 75mm gun.

The second casemate in the old German defence complex has been converted into a holiday home.

was vital to the assault of 231 Brigade...'

At 1520 hours, 50 Division were reporting to HQ XXX Corps that '1 Hants have got Cabane'. According to the acting CO Major David Warren, the battery was 'captured with about thirty prisoners and only slight casualties, so they [D Company] were sent on to the Radar Station'.

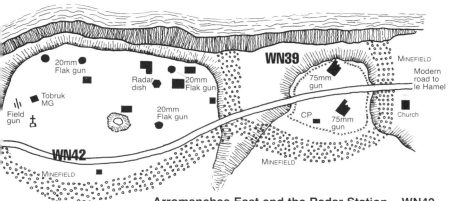

Arromanches East and the Radar Station – WN42

Four hundred yards ahead of D Company, on a plateau immediately east of Arromanches, lay a radar station and an infantry platoon's defensive position. The Arromanches Radar Station was a part of a dense network of such stations along the Atlantic, Channel and North Sea Coasts and was also deployed in various inland belts. The Germans developed radar independently of the British and had by 1944 deployed several types of radar. Some were designed to detect shipping and direct the fire of shore batteries once an invasion force had closed into the French coast, while others were deployed in response to the RAF's night bomber offensive. Sets such as the *Freya*, manned by *Luftwaffe* personnel, were used to direct night fighters against British bombers. Other well-known radar sites in Normandy are at Douvres and on Mont Pincon.

The intelligence information passed on to the Hampshires was as follows:

> *'The station is surrounded by a double belt of wire fifteen to eighteen feet thick, and probably containing mines. Local protection of this position is afforded by several open MG pits and a probable pillbox, covering the shore and landwards.'*

The position was taken quickly and efficiently, with naval and artillery firepower again demonstrating its effectiveness in stunning the enemy.

> *'The Radar Station at 855864 was captured with about forty prisoners, with only slight casualties being suffered, and, after a 15 min bombardment*

The Giant Würtzburg at Arromanches, with the Mulberry Harbour taking shape behind it.

The view eastwards from the Radar Station to JIG.

from a destroyer followed by a 10 minute concentration by 147 Fd Regt.'
The mainly *Luftwaffe and Kriegsmarine* occupants of the Radar Station did
not put up much resistance as the Hampshires advanced up the hill
towards them, accompanied by a troop of Sherwood Rangers' Shermans. A
few enemy escaped downhill into Arromanches, but most surrendered and
a few were killed as D Company cleared the bunkers. In the confines of a
bunker, where the enemy is met at close quarters in the dark, the tense
infantrymen took no risks and shot first. However, by 1740 hours, the
Tactical HQ of 50 Division, who were now ashore, were signalling to XXX
Corps HQ that '231 Bde are fighting on outskirts of Arromanches and Ryes.
Over an hour later, at 1900 hours, 231 Brigade's war diary recorded that '1
Hamps capture OP and radar stn east of Arromanches'. Major Mott records
that in a subsequent check of the station, the infantrymen found the
German 'canteen was undamaged until the troops got there, and the ration
store the same, as were the officers' quarters, which contained some useful
kit'.

Having been initially delayed by fire from this dominating ridge that
barred the way to Arromanches, D Company found that breaking through
the German positions was relatively easy. Looking at the battle as a whole,
1 Hampshire's commanders contrasted the protracted and bitter fighting in
le Hamel, where the Germans had been missed by the bombardment, with
the swift capture of the Arromanches positions, where the enemy had been
accurately engaged by artillery. On the first day of the Normandy
Campaign, the power of properly co-ordinated and directed artillery was
already evident.

From the Radar Station, the Hampshires' next objective was the
defences on the cliff immediately to the east of Arromanches. The position
was described to the Battalion as,

'an infantry strongpoint consisting of two pillboxes for MGs, and three
or four MG positions connected by a trench system'.
By D-Day, there was also a field-gun dug in on the cliff top, positioned with
arcs of fire to cover the landward approaches to Arromanches. However,
following a short bombardment,

> *'the position at 843867 was liquidated, with the capture of about 20 prisoners, there being no real resistance and no casualties to the assaulting troops.'*

From this position, the soldiers of D Company could look down the steep hillside into Arromanches.

The Liberation of Arromanches

Allied plans attempted to ensure that Arromanches suffered as little battle damage as possible, as the small town was planned to be the main entry point for British logistics – the Mulberry Harbour. In order not to prevent the foreshore being quickly brought into use, the town was not to be directly attacked. Before the Hampshires could enter Arromanches, the platoon position on the western cliff had to be captured. However, D Company were exposed and were holding a large portion of ground from Cabane to the outskirts of Arromanches and, therefore, would have to await reinforcement before clearing the town. While holding their position, the Hampshiremen were sniped at from Arromanches; however, a few rounds from a destroyer, accurately directed by an FOB, quietened the Germans.

Major Warren, having secured le Hamel, pushed on the greatly thinned ranks of B and C Companies. He ordered them:

> *'... to move to the Radar Station down the road Asnelles sur Mer – St Cômte-de-Fresne cutting across the fields to the church. Companies were to disperse in the area of the half-troop position and an O* [Orders] *Group was to rendezvous at the Giant Wurtzburg tower. All the fields on the road to St Cômte-de-Fresne were marked with white mine warning notices, but although no conclusions had been drawn from the two different types of warning notices it was decided that the troops must go through the fields.*
>
> *'The O Group was held at the Radar Station where there was an excellent view of the next objective* [Arromanches West]. *The plan was that D Company should move down and around the southern end of Arromanches and take the position from the rear. Supporting fire would be a 15-minute bombardment from a destroyer, followed by a ten-minute concentration by the SP regiment. B and C Companies would support the attack with small arms fire from the forward edge of the radar station position, overlooking Arromanches. On capture of their objective, D Company would send one platoon to deal with the OP ...* [on the cliff further west].'

Again the power of naval gunfire support and artillery worked and the position was overcome with, according to Major Warren, 'no real resistance and about twenty prisoners were taken, with no casualties suffered'.

It would seem that the clearance of the wider Arromanches West position was not as thorough as it could have been. Brigadier Walter of the

The field gun position above Arromanches then and now.

Arromanches West

Mulberry Harbour construction organization that came ashore on D+1, recorded that:

> 'We ended the day by bivouacking in a wood to the west of Arromanches as dusk was falling. We dispersed early next morning [8 June] but about mid-morning there came sounds of battle from the west of the town. Later it transpired that a party of about sixty Germans had emerged from underground passages below where we had bivouacked the night before and were engaged by such Port Construction Force troops as could be mustered who, with the aid of a tank, killed some but took forty-seven prisoners.'

The actual liberation of Arromanches quickly followed afterwards. At 2000 hours, Major Mott led B and C Companies forward. He recalled:

> 'We were to meet some tanks in case we needed help. They never arrived, so I went in [from the south] without them. The only opposition was from a dog, presumably a Boche one, his three brave masters followed him with a flag. Arromanches was full of French people. Flowers came out and tricolours and Union Jacks.'

Other accounts, however, record that the French people were walking about 'just as if it were an exercise back in England' and generally getting in the way of rounding up the Germans. Major Mott may have had an easy entry but some enemy action must have prompted the comment in the war diary that 'Enemy 88mm [they were 77mm] guns and *Spandau* teams, which put up a determined resistance, were ultimately wiped out.' By 2100 hours, Arromanches was secure in 231 Brigade's hands.

The day's fighting had cost 1 Hampshire five officers killed and eleven wounded, with casualties amongst other ranks totalling 166 men killed or wounded.

With the capture of Arromanches, 231 Brigade could justifiably be proud of its achievements. Unlike elsewhere on D-Day, the Brigade had completed nearly all its allocated tasks and had done so against the high-quality 352nd Division, whose presence had contributed to the near-disaster at OMAHA Beach. With 56 Infantry Brigade pushing south from Ryes towards Bayeux, the focus of 231 Brigade's operations lay to the west.

The Longues-sur-Mer Battery and Port-en-Bessin had to be subdued and the link-up with the Americans to be made.

Barrie, taken prisoner at Arromanches and conscripted into 1 Hampshire. Renamed 'Dog Fritz', he became their mascot.

130

CHAPTER EIGHT

THE LONGUES SUR MER BATTERY

The Longues-sur-Mer Battery, located in the very centre of the invasion area, was as every bit as dangerous as either the Merville Battery, on the British flank or the St Marcouf Battery north of UTAH Beach. Its guns were sited to cover the sea to its front out to a range of fourteen miles, which included the approaches to GOLD, JUNO and OMAHA Beaches that were on D-Day crowded with craft of all types.

Unlike other batteries in the central invasion area, Longues-sur-Mer was built, manned and commanded by the *Kriegsmarine*. Work had started in September 1943 to produce heavy concrete casemates for the four C/36 152mm *torpedobootskanone*, made in the Skoda Works at Pilsen. These highly effective guns, which had been dismounted from a destroyer of the blockaded *Kriegsmarine*, had a much greater range and throw weight than their field gun equivalents. The type M272 casemates housing the guns were of a different design to *Wehrmacht* constructions, the chief difference being the wide foundations that gave the casemates greater stability in the event of a near miss by large bombs or shells. In addition, in line with normal *Kriegsmarine* practice, most of the four hundred rounds of ammunition per gun were kept in magazine shelters to the rear of each

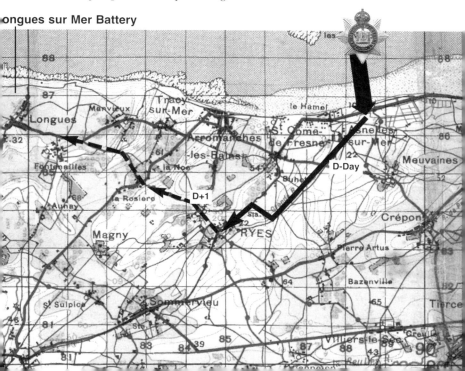

ongues sur Mer Battery

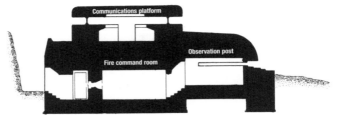

**The M262
Longues-sur-Mer
Battery
Command Post**

0 1 2 3 4 5 6 7

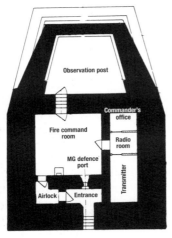

Observation post

Fire command
room

Commander's
office

Radio
room

MG defence
port

Transmitter

Airlock   Entrance

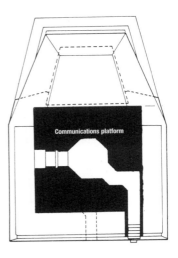

Communications platform

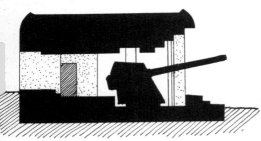

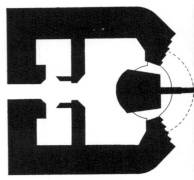

**Cross section and plan of
the M272 casemates at the
Longues-sur-Mer Battery**

10 YARDS

casemate. This contrasted with *Wehrmacht* practice where the first line ammunition was stored in the gun casemates. On the cliff top, three hundred yards in front of the battery, stands the equally massive M262 command post casemate, where the battery's optical range-finder was located, along with radio and line communications from outside. As Colonel Ocker of 352nd Division complained in his post-war questioning, the battery was under command of the *Kriegsmarine* until the Allied landing began; as a result, little co-ordinated fire control planning had taken place. This was typical of Hitler's web of duplicated and overlapping

Longues-sur-Mer Battery under construction, prior to being bombed.

A casemate belonging to the Kriegsmarine battery at Longues-sur -Mer clearly showing the near-misses by the RAF.

responsibilities that was designed to divide and rule and did so much to undermine the operational effectiveness of the German forces.

Both Resistance and air recce closely monitored the construction of the massive casemates over the months before D-Day, as its guns were a significant concern to the naval planners. However, of equal importance to 2 Devon, who were to deliver the ground attack on the battery, was the proliferation of surrounding minefields and wire. The April 1944 edition of 231 Brigade's Intelligence Summary described the battery, which was still under construction:

> *'A thin belt of wire – probably double apron – contains the strong point, but is thickened up at the main defences overlooking the beach, and covering an exit up the cliff. A track leads up from the beach, but is blocked by a wall. The defences consist of weapon pits and trench systems, with concrete shelters to the rear of them. Work is still progressing on the gun site. ... The mine field consists of zig-zag belts of four to eight rows of mines; no two adjoining belts appear to have the same layout, and the width of the belt varies from 30ft to as much as 110 ft in the case of belts with eight rows.'*

In addition, after the battery's capture, the Devons found that shells, primed for remote detonation, had been positioned on the cliff to deal with attack from the sea. As more intelligence came in during May, the increasing seriousness of the task facing 2 Devon became more apparent. While the casemate neared completion, the ground defences were thickened up. In total, there were fourteen concrete structures – either shelters or weapons pits. The latter contained machine-guns and, according to the report of a Special (naval gunfire) Observer Party, 'two 20 mm guns for ground and air defence, three 80mm medium mortar pits and a searchlight'.

Unlike Merville, the Longues-sur-Mer battery was not to be subject to an airborne attack before the landings, despite being a more significant threat. The airborne drop at Merville was partly due to the fact that it was coincidentally in the centre of 6th Airborne Division's area and, secondly, Merville could not be directly observed and engaged by Allied warships. As a *Kriegsmarine* coastal battery, Longues-sur-Mer was sited to engage targets out to sea, over open sights if necessary. Whereas, sited inland, Merville's task was to neutralize troops landing on the beach, with fire being directed by an observer. However, the Allied navies were confident that they could successfully engage the Longues-sur-Mer casemates on the cliff-top and prevent the battery from inflicting significant damage.

The first phase of the Allied plan to deal with the threat posed by Longues-sur-Mer was bombing, in the weeks before the invasion, to slow construction. In the days before D-Day, the Battery was heavily bombed on the nights of 28/29 May and again on 3/4 June. A total of 1,500 tonnes of bombs was dropped. The effect of the 28/29 May bombing impressed the Devons and Colonel Nevill recalled seeing air photographs of the battery:

> 'As I was about to go on board, I was met by the Brigade Commander who said, "I have got here photos which will delight your eyes. The RAF are apologetic about them, saying that of course it is only their first bombing of the place; they hope to do much better later!" We could hardly believe our eyes. The whole area looked a mass of craters. The photographs were passed rapidly round the ship and the atmosphere was "Well, if the RAF bomb every enemy position like that, the whole party will be a complete picnic". We no longer felt as anxious about Longues.'

See photo page 133

This, however, did not represent the end of the aerial bombardment. While the Allied airborne divisions were dropping shortly after midnight on 5/6 June, the battery was deluged by five hundred tons of bombs and was later attacked by five squadrons of heavy bombers from H-40 to H+10. The next stage of the attack was to be a bombardment by the Royal Navy's HMS *Ajax* with her eight 6-inch guns. She would engage the casemates in a traditional gun duel that was designed to neutralize the battery until it could be cleared by 2 Devon, sometime after H+5 hours on D-Day.

D-Day Action

There is a degree of controversy between the British and French over the naval engagement of Longues-sur-Mer. However, naval logs of the ships concerned provide a precise record of the action. At 0500 hours, HMS *Ajax* was lying at anchor six nautical miles to the north of Longues-sur-Mer.

Captain Weld, searching the coastline through his binoculars in the early dawn light, saw the low silhouette of the battery on the cliff top. At 0530 hours (sunrise minus forty minutes), he ordered his eight 6-inch guns to open fire. At first, there was no response. However, the battery opened fire, initially at the destroyer USS *Emmons* at 0537 hours, but switched its fire to the battleship USS *Arkansas* lying off OMAHA at a range of ten miles. *Arkansas* and the French cruiser *Georges Leygues* joined *Ajax's* engagement, firing twenty twelve-inch and one hundred and ten five-inch shells, and the battery fell silent. At 0557, the battery again opened fire, this time to the east, at the anchored HMS *Bulolo* off GOLD, with the first rounds from Number 3 and 4 guns straddling the target. *Bulolo* was a prime target, being the Naval Force G's flagship and 50th Division's HQ ship and, therefore, a vital nerve centre. She quickly weighed anchor and moved seaward. At 0605 hours Number 1 and 2 guns re-engaged *Arkansas* and the two French cruisers. In response, FFS *Montcalm* joined HMS *Ajax* in her redoubled rate of fire and, by 0620 hours, the battery was again silenced. Over the next two hours, the battery came into action again several times, engaging targets in the GOLD area. HMS *Argonaut* joined *Ajax* and fired twenty-nine and one hundred and fifty rounds respectively before the battery was silenced at 0845 hours. The guns in casemates 3 and 4 were knocked out, while numbers 1 and 2 were damaged.

By late afternoon, the *Kriegsmarine* gunners had repaired Number 1 gun, which, because the open front was facing slightly to the west, had been more difficult for *Ajax* to engage effectively. This gun opened fire on shipping off OMAHA, where the battle was only just swinging in the Americans' favour. *George Leygues*, under command of Naval Bombardment Force C, replied. There was a terse exchange of Aldis Lamp

HMS Ajax in action on D-Day against Longues-sur-Mer Battery.

The Longues-sur-Mer Battery after the bombing on 28/29 May 1944.

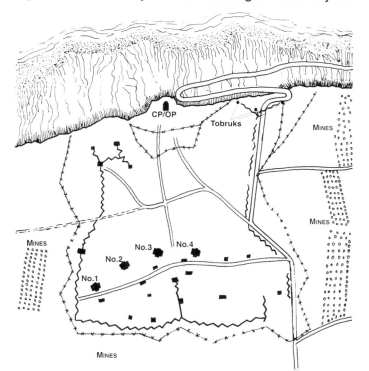

signals between Captain Weld and Admiral Jaujard, the former claiming the battery as *Ajax's* exclusive target. The French were not impressed and *George Leygues* continued to engage! Number 1 gun was finally put out of action at 1800 hours, by the fire of both ships.

From the number of empty cylinders in the casemates, it is estimated that the battery fired approximately one hundred and fifty rounds during the course of D-Day. Without the air and naval bombardment, the effect of these shells, and 1,050 rounds found in the battery's magazines, would have been highly significant, especially off OMAHA, where the battle hung in the balance for most of the day. Commander Edwards attributes Longues-sur-Mer's neutralization 'to some exhibition shooting on the part of *Ajax*, which will long be quoted as an instance of amazing gunnery by a ship against a shore battery'. 2 Devon's ground attack planned for D-Day did not take place as scheduled. The delay on the beach and more determined resistance than expected caused the battalion to halt at Ryes for the night.

The Attack on D+1

At 0530 hours, B Company led 2 Devon's advance westward from Ryes to the Masse de Cradalle, which was occupied without opposition at 0700 hours. C Company rejoined the battalion from its overnight location in la Rosière and took the lead towards the village of Longues with Lieutenant Colonel Nevill's Tactical HQ and the remainder of the battalion following. The commanding officer recorded that:

> *'When we got to within 3,000 yards of the village we had our first view of the battery itself. Lieutenant Frank Pease, now commanding C Company, and I, looking through our field glasses, wondered whether in fact it was occupied. Our doubts were soon dispelled by the appearance of two Germans walking slowly across the area. At this moment, the Brigade Commander arrived to say that HMS Ajax and a squadron of fighter-bombers would be available to support the attack. As we knew the strength of the position was still formidable, in spite of the RAF softening-up, we gladly made use of their assistance. It was decided that Ajax would fire [from 0815] until 0845 hours, at which time the squadron of fighter-bombers would blast the place for five minutes. The MG Platoon of 2 Cheshire, under Capt Bill Williams, would give direct support to the infantry attack, timed to take place at 0900 hours.'*

C Company were to deliver the attack. Lieutenant David Holdsworth recalled that the bombardment was 'a marvellous spectacle, and we wondered how anybody could still be alive in the great concrete-faced battery'. The plan was to attack through the village, astride the road, where the minefields appeared to be fewer. Lieutenant Holdsworth described C Company's advance, which began at 0852 hours, 'accompanied by a party

The massive M262 Command Post casemate on the cliff edge was a key part of the battery. The holes in the concrete were cast as a part of the camouflage screen.

of Brigade and Divisional staff officers who had come along for the fun of it':

> 'This was a set piece battle and, apparently, a lot depended upon it. The two leading platoons and the acting company commander [Lieutenant Pease] made their tortuous way towards the battery. There was no sound from it, either because the enemy were holding their fire or because they were dead.'

There is no mention in any accounts of casualties from mines during the attack. Presumably, a high proportion of the minefields were dummy and the Royal Navy and RAF bombardment had sympathetically detonated many others. It is highly likely that, with landmines not being a normal *Kriegsmarine* inventory item, the number laid was limited. Lieutenant Holdsworth continued:

> 'In the rear came my platoon. To my surprise, the two leading platoons made their way beyond the place from which they were expected to carry out

the final assault. My platoon was just about level with it. The acting Company Commander realized this. Time was against a complete reorganization to carry out the original assault plan by 0900 hours. There was only one thing to do. And he did it. He ordered an about turn. The effect was to make my platoon into the lead platoon and, therefore, commit it to immediate attack.

'Faced with barbed wire encircling the whole of the approach to the battery, and with those wretched "Achtung Minen!" signs generously scattered round the area, we felt pitifully inadequate to the demands of the situation. The only pleasant feature about the whole affair was the fact that no-one was firing at us from the battery.

'We advanced to the wire in a very open formation. Still there was no sound from the enemy. Gingerly we stepped over the wire and down one of the criss-cross paths. At that moment one of the massive iron doors of the battery swung open. Out came the enemy with white flags held out in front of them.'

However, not all of the *Kriegsmarine* gunners were prepared to surrender so easily and machine-gun and rifle fire was directed at the Devons from across the battery. This complicated and slowed down the clearance of the positions, which was a labyrinth of bunkers, blown-in trenches and a few tunnels. With some enemy still active, the Devons had to assume the worst and methodically clear the battery. In doing so, they suffered a number of casualties, including Captain Nobby Clark, who was killed near the German command post on the cliff edge, which held out longer than other parts of the battery. Private Kerslake recalled:

'We attacked one of the gun bunkers, where we had to go round to the front as we couldn't make any impression on the heavy door at the back. As we went around the mounds of earth, we came under fire from a very heavy calibre machine gun [probably one of the 20mm guns] *and only survived as there were plenty of craters from near-misses to hide in.*

After my experience of the landing the day before, I was not looking forward to clearing the gun bunker and, even though it was hot, I was in a cold sweat. Under covering fire we went in. After the bright daylight, we couldn't see anything. There were shots that dangerously ricocheted off the walls. I never did find out if they were ours or theirs. We went through the bunker, we had been warned not to use grenades, as we would have in normal buildings, as we could have exploded ammunitions and ourselves with it. We reached the back door and opened it and I nearly got shot by a very young lad from our platoon who was on his own; very jumpy and very white.'

At 1053, the battery was reported as captured; in addition to the naval guns, a 76mm field gun was captured, along with its crew, dug-in within the perimeter. Following the German surrender and the taking of ninety prisoners, out of a reported strength of 184 *Kriegsmarine* gunners, Lieutenant Holdsworth explained:

'Tension eased immediately. The enemy walked down one of the paths towards us. We walked up the same path towards them. The battery was ours. Over a hundred enemy soldiers came out of the concrete-covered chambers inside the battery, all with their hands up. Inside the chamber was a smell, which I can only describe as the smell of human fear. Having witnessed the bombardment to which they had been subjected, it wasn't really surprising that they had surrendered. I would have done the same.'

A Devon recalls a chance meeting at the battery with one of the German prisoners many years later:

'The German told us he was a sailor not a soldier but he had never been to sea. This we had not known and I began to feel for him when he explained how the RAF had hit his battery regularly and how they felt like sitting ducks on the cliff top. The sight of the invasion fleet was intimidating and it was only our Navy's gunfire that prevented many of them from running away! They had no instruction what to do but the officers said that they were to fight us "Tommies" when we came but the final bombardment convinced several groups to surrender.'

British Army soldiers visiting the battery occupy the gun crew's positions. Note the massive breech.

Lieutenant Holdsworth described the aftermath of the attack:

'Having disposed of the battery successfully and, to their relief, without much trouble, my platoon displayed many of the usual symptoms of a victorious army. Inside the fortified central chamber were pictures of Hitler and other German leaders. Possibly because we hadn't had to shoot anyone in anger, mixed feelings of relief and achievement found expression in the destruction of all the pictures hanging on the walls.

Fortunately, this mood of destruction didn't last long, and within a few minutes we collected ourselves together and formed again into a fairly recognizable, disciplined unit. Some pockets bulged with loot but, on the whole, we had behaved as well as any soldier can be expected to behave on these occasions.

It had been exciting and, thank goodness, an entirely successful military operation for us, and we now indulged in noisy high spirits. Back we went to our company transport.'

Overall, the Longues-sur-Mer Battery, arguably a formidable fortification, did not prove to be as dangerous as was thought. The weight of well co-ordinated Allied firepower was brought to bear and effectively neutralized the enemy guns and gunners. So shocked were the Germans that 2 Devon's 'attack' was more a mopping-up operation than a true attack.

Casemate No.2 is always a popular spot for a group photograph.

CHAPTER NINE

OPERATION AUBERY
47 COMMANDO'S ATTACK ON PORT-EN-BESSIN

47 Commando Royal Marines was formed at the Depot Barracks in Dorchester on 1st August 1943, under Lieutenant Colonel CF Phillips, from a hard core of experienced commandos from across the Corps. Having completed basic training, the unit moved to the Commando Training Depot at Achnacarry, where the Marines earned their coveted green berets following a high standard of military training – a course that tested their determination, fitness and stamina.

Rapidly emerging as one of the best Commando units, 47 were allocated, arguably, the most difficult objective of the eight commando units in action on D-Day. Port-en-Bessin was a small port in the centre of the fifteen-mile gap between 231 Brigade on GOLD Beach and 1st (US) Division at the eastern end of OMAHA. 50th Division's historian described the Commandos' objective:

> 'The small fishing port formed the right-hand boundary of the 50th Division sector, and its capture as early as possible was considered vital to the security of the XXX Corps' right flank and to effectively link up with the 1st US Division, which was our right-hand neighbour. The town is in a hollow between cliffs approximately two hundred feet in height. It is fronted by a promenade and backed by closely-packed houses and narrow streets. Towards the south-east part of town, the houses are less closely packed and are interspersed by gardens and small fields. Approaches to the town are very open and exposed, particularly the south-east approaches.

> 'Like other ports on the Normandy coast, Port-en-Bessin was well defended by a system of strong-points on the cliffs overlooking the town and included emplaced guns sited to fire seawards, guns and machine-guns in open embrasures capable of firing both to sea and inland, trench systems, surrounded by minefields and wire at the various strong-points, and fortified houses and pillboxes on the mole and in the town itself.

> 'The Garrison was thought to be approximately one company, with some fifty naval personnel in the town and port defences.'

The resources required to carry out a direct amphibious assault on the heavily defended port were too great to entertain. Therefore, 47 Commando would be under command for landing of 231 Brigade and land behind the assault infantry. Once concentrated ashore, they were to strike across enemy-held country, on foot, to reach Port-en-Bessin, ten miles away. Lieutenant Colonel Nevill describes an incident at the first 50th Division Overlord briefing in April 1944:

> 'There was a tense moment at the Divisional Commander's Conference when General Graham asked Colonel Phillips whether in addition to his other tasks, he could mop up the odd position, which was known to exist between Port-en-Bessin and Longues. Colonel Phillips replied that General Dempsey had personally instructed him to capture the Port; that he would then be relieved by 50 Division, thus enabling him and his unit to return to England (laughter). He respectfully regretted therefore that he would be unable to assist in this small matter (loud laughter).'

47 Commando's mission was eventually confirmed in 231 Infantry Brigade's operation order as follows:

PHASE IV: STRAWBERRY

> '*R Marines* – 47 RM Commando will land approx H plus 2 hours on JIG Sector under Op Control of 231 Inf Bde and will capture Port-en-Bessin.
>
> **Phase 1.** Land H+2. Assembly area just W of la Rosière by H+3½ via check pt 876859.
>
> **Phase 2.** Seize Pt 72 by H+5½, later if en positions have to be bypassed.
>
> **Phase 3.** Capture high ground 50m feature E of the basin in Port-en-

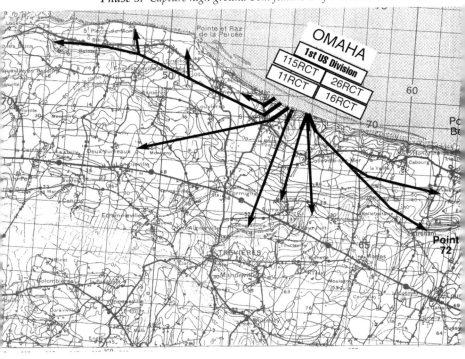

Bessin, not before H+6½, subject to time of air support request.
    Phase 4. *Capture of high ground Pt 57 – W of Port-en-Bessin.'*
In common with the other units attacking coastal objectives, a considerable range of fire support was available to 47 Commando. This included one US destroyer that was to suppress the defences of Port-en-Bessin up to H+6½ hours. In addition, a Forward Officer Bombardment, who would accompany 47, was to bring fire to bear from the French cruiser *Montcalm's* nine six-inch guns, which were on call from H+4, in a forty-minute bombardment. A Forward Observation Officer (FOO) from 147 Field Regiment was to have fire from his Regiment's 25-pounders available from H+3½. Finally, a US Artillery FOO, having landed at OMAHA, was planned to join 47 in area of Point 72. Superimposed on this very heavy naval and ground fire were close air support sorties for fifteen minutes before 47's attack on the main enemy position on the high ground to the east of the port. By any measure, this was an impressive range of firepower.

Landing and Breakout

    Captain Jefereys's J4 Commando and Ranger Naval Assault Group RN were to cross the Channel in LCIs from Warsash. However, 47 embarked on two of the larger 'mother ships'. They were to cross on two ships, SS *Victoria* and transfer to the six LCAs of 508 Assault Flotilla and HMS *Princess Josephine Charlotte's* (502 Assault Flotilla) eight LCAs. The crossing

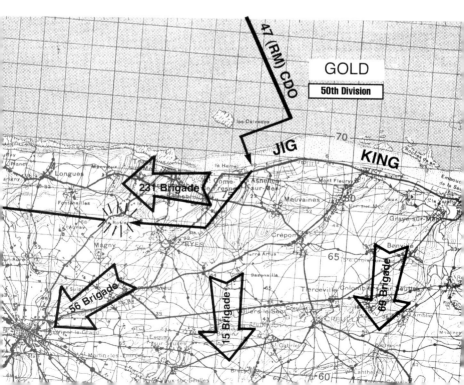

and transfer to their LCAs went well and the run-in to the beach began. However, Colonel Phillips, unlike most of 231 Brigade, realized that he was heading for the wrong point on the beach. Lieutenant Peter Winter RM recalled the final run into JIG Green:

> *'Our fourteen landing craft came inshore in line astern but the CO did something he shouldn't have and turned parallel to the coast to get to our correct landing beach and made a good target for the Germans.'*

47 Commando landed at 0930 hours; the worst time possible for mines, sea conditions and congestion in the water and on the beach. The fourteen LCAs had to make their way through the uncleared and mined beach obstacles in a heavy sea. Five were sunk and another five were damaged, causing casualties and capsizes. Lieutenant Peter Winter continued:

> *'My landing craft hit a mine and I was knocked unconscious for a while. When I woke up, I found myself in the water. I had a broken leg and a broken arm and attempted to swim ashore but only ended up going around in circles. A sergeant saw me and, despite the awfulness of the situation, said, "You won't get anywhere fast like that, Sir. You had better think of something better." I eventually made it ashore where my MOA [Marine Officer's Assistant – batman], Marine Woodgate, met me on the beach with the words, "I thought you'd like a cup of tea, Sir". I can tell you that no cup of tea ever tasted better. The doctor could do little for us wounded, as he had few orderlies and they had lost all their medical equipment when their landing craft was sunk. It took me three days to reach hospital in England.'*

Amongst those who, unwounded, found themselves in the sea was Sergeant Donald Gardner.

> *'We swam ashore, about fifty yards, under machine-gun fire and at one point I heard someone say, "Perhaps we're intruding, this seems to be a private beach".'*

Humour in adversity has always been a feature of life in the commandos. Many others from the four mined craft were able to swim ashore but, invariably, they had lost their eighty-eight pounds of weapons and equipment in the process. Once ashore, 47 'concentrated at the back of the beach during clarification of situation ... Mortar fire and shelling of the beach continued'.

Initially, only about three hundred of the four hundred and seventy Marines were present. Amongst the missing was Lieutenant Colonel Phillips. In an often unrecorded loss, only two of the fourteen LCAs, each crewed by two Marines, made it back to the 'mother ships' SS *Victoria* and HMS *Princess Josephine Charlotte*.

The citation for Major Patrick Donnell's Croix de Guerre with Vermilion Star describes how, with the CO forward on a recce, he gathered the Commando together and led them off the beach, reporting to Brigadier

Stanier that they had lost much of their equipment. Advancing behind the Devons, 47 Commando started its reorganization in the area of Buhot, which, at the time, was far from secure. Soldiers of 231 Brigade donated items of equipment, as recalled by Private Powis of 2 Devons:

'A drenched and dripping Commando unit now joined us at the side of the road, they were almost completely unarmed and looked a very sad sight. They explained that they had come in on the high tide and their landing craft had either hit the ramps or bottle mines, so they were forced to throw off their equipment and swim ashore. Having armed themselves with whatever they could from dead soldiers, they welcomed anything we could spare in the way of armaments and ammunition. I gave them one of my two fifty-round bandoliers of rifle ammunition, a grenade and two magazines for the Bren gun.

'The Commando went along the road furnishing themselves with small arms and ammunition from the German and British soldiers now lying dead there. They filtered through the leading Devon company, engaging the Germans with their captured and borrowed weapons.'

Delays in getting away from the beach area had been considerable but, having reorganized, the commandos now had to slip through the enemy positions on the ridge of high ground south of Arromanches, rather than following up behind 231 Brigade. While crossing the ridge, the Royal Marines 'had one brush and two small battles with the Germans'. However, on reaching the area where they were originally planned to have assembled, the Commando found that la Rosière was still occupied by a weak company of German infantry.

An attack was quickly arranged, without fire support, as most of the radios had been lost with the other heavy equipment during the landing. B

Five of the LCAs carrying men of 47 Commando were sunk by mines on the run-in with the loss of forty commandos. 47 Commando landing at 0950 hours were to break through the enemy lines and capture Port-en-Bessin.

Troop led the attack under the cover of smoke laid by the Commando's remaining 2-inch mortars.

Marine 'Shock' Kendrick was attempting to treat the wounded:

'A machine-gun opened up on us injuring some of the lads. "Shock!" The cry rang out from one of the wounded. As I tended to the lad, I realized I couldn't do all the necessary first aid in a prone position, but as soon as I stood up the machine gun opened up again. I could see the bullets hitting the hedge but, as they came nearer to me, the gun must have lifted. Although the firing continued, the bullets were flying about above my head. We put in a flank attack and captured the machine-gun crew. The gunner had a right shoulder injury. I had to treat him and when I finished, he hugged me. A scout car with six Germans in it suddenly rounded a bend in the road. We dealt with it. Soon afterwards, we heard a horse galloping down the lane and as it came into view we saw that it had a German rider. Sergeant Hooper stepped into the lane and fired his Tommy gun. The horse galloped off with the dead body still on his back.'

At 1900 hours, it was reported to Corps Headquarters, aboard HMS *Bulolo*, that 47 Commando was 'now in la Rosière' but it was not until 1945 hours that 47 was ready to set off towards Port-en-Bessin, having suffered eleven casualties. However, they had taken every useful enemy weapon and piece of ammunition from the dead, the wounded and from prisoners, in order to make up for their losses on landing. These were not the kind of soldiers to be deflected from their mission by mere administrative inconveniences.

Commander Kenneth Edwards in his Royal Naval history of Operation Neptune records that:

'After fighting another battle with German detachments, and crossing a small river, the Commando arrived on Point 72, a prominent hill immediately south of Port-en-Bessin. There they dug in for the night. They were in a dangerous position, between the defences of Port-en-Bessin and a fortified German camp at [Chateau] Fosse Soucy, about a mile south of Point 72.'

The Plan Revised – D+1

At dawn, 47 sent patrols westward to locate the Americans, who should by now have closed up to the Army boundary, just to the west of Point 72. The commandos did not learn until much later that, also facing 352nd Division, the 1st US Division, at OMAHA beach, had fared badly. Without contacting the Americans, the commandos had to face the prospect of attacking the port and its dominating cliff-top strong-points with fire support, from the Allied navies, artillery and airforces, co-ordinated over its single remaining radio. The plan to assault the flanking cliff-top positions, avoiding the town, was abandoned as impractical. Instead, Lieutenant Colonel Phillips decided that the Commando would bypass the

A commando Bren gun team covers the advance of the rest of
their troop.

small strong point on the southern outskirts of the town and infiltrate into the town. Once in Port-en-Bessin, the commandos would clear the town and port area before attacking the defences on the cliffs to the east and west. However, before the attack could begin, the Marines needed more ammunition. To their support came 522 Company Royal Army Service Corps. Captain Brian Lindon's Military Cross citation records the re-supply operation:

'On 7 Jun 44 it was essential that the 47 Commandos, who were assaulting Port-en-Bessin, be supplied with ammunition, water and food, although well in enemy territory. Captain Lindon set out with two 3-ton vehicles to perform this task.

'He passed through the leading elements of 2 Devons in the area of Longues being told by them that the enemy were ahead. In spite of this he carried on in order to contact 47 Commando at Point 72 near Escures.

'Although he had to run the gauntlet of considerable small arms fire from enemy infantry who were flanking his route, his vehicle being hit several times, he succeeded not only in the delivery of his loads, but in safely getting back the empty vehicles.

'It was largely due to Captain Lindon's determination to get these essential supplies through, his disregard for personal safety and skilful handling of his vehicles, that 47 Commando received the necessary ammunition to enable them to continue the operation in which they were involved.'

Actions such as this by logistic troops can often be overlooked but in this case, it is clear that without the vital ammunition, 47 Commando would not have been able to take the town of Port-en-Bessin.

Re-supply completed, the attack would begin at 1600 hours. However, destroyers began engaging the port and its defences at 1400 hours, with the cruiser HMS *Emerald* of Bombarding Force K turning her seven 6-inch guns landward and sending her 100-pound shells into the German positions at 1500 hours. Ten minutes before H-hour, three squadrons of RAF Typhoons 'came in and plastered the three German positions with extreme accuracy' and finally, the 25-pounders of 431 Battery of 147 (Essex Yeomanry) Field Regiment RA fired HE and smoke. The commandos had been joined by a FOO, who controlled the fire of the guns that were in positions near le Hamel.

The Attack on Port-en-Bessin

As the advance began, the commandos were engaged by *Spandaus* firing on them from their left rear. This fire caused some casualties and a delay while the enemy were neutralised. Barring the way into Port-en-Bessin from Point 72 was the Southern Strongpoint, which was described as being:

'... on the slope of the high ground south of Port-en-Bessin, covering the southern approaches to the town and docks. It is surrounded by a thick belt of wire, with two small gaps. There is one pillbox facing NE, and one concrete shelter. Several weapon pits give all-round fire, and a trench system is dug just south of the pillbox.'

This position was, however, plastered with extreme accuracy by artillery, as 47 bypassed it to the east. The Commando entered the town and was immediately embroiled in 'confused street fighting'. Fighting their way through the narrow roads and stone buildings was a slow business. However, A Troop had bypassed the worst of the fighting and been able to mount an attack up the slope to the west of the town. The fighting was not at all straightforward, with mines, wire, trenches and bunkers having to be cleared, but the German coastal troops were no match for the determined commandos. At 2030 hours, about a hundred Germans surrendered. However, Lieutenant Peter Winter RM recounted that:

'During the attack on the Western Hill, Cpl Amos stopped to put a first field dressing on a wounded friend. While he was doing this, he was taken prisoner and marched off to a bunker where, on the wall, was Hitler's order that "All Commandos are to be shot". Corporal Amos spent a very uncomfortable night with a Gestapo man standing around supervising. As our final attack on the Eastern Hill was going in and the Marines could be seen on the German position, the Gestapo man, "seeing the writing on the wall", left the bunker. As soon as he had gone, the German military commander got out a cigar and offered it to Corporal Amos, saying, "We would very much like to surrender". Corporal Amos fell the Germans into three ranks and with a large flag marched the Germans down the hill and that was that. Except when he got to the bottom of the hill, his Troop

The view of Port-en-Bassin from 47 Commando's 'firm base' on Point 72.

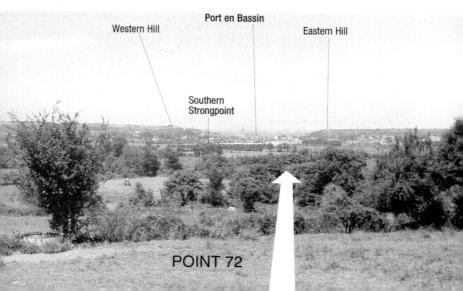

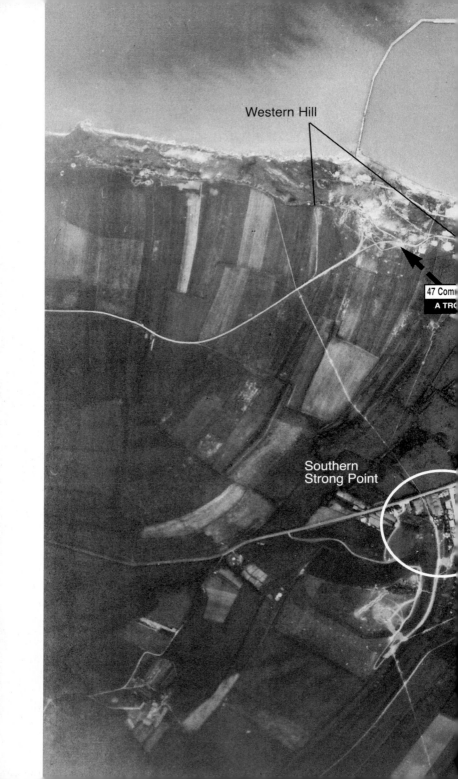

Western Hill

47 Com
A TRO

Southern
Strong Point

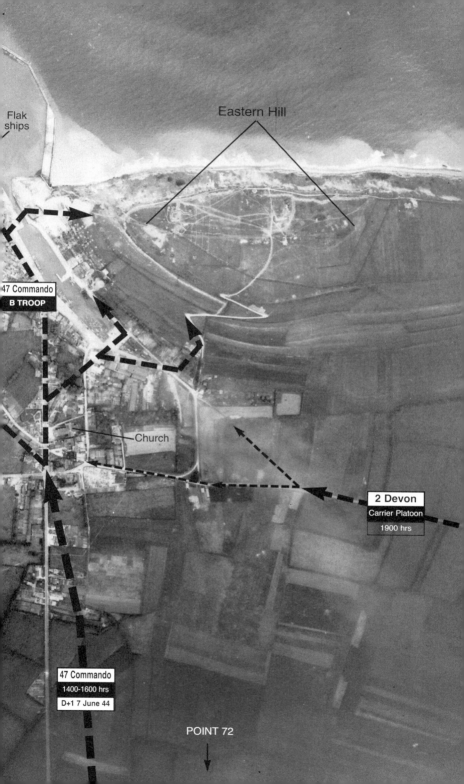

Flak
ships

Eastern Hill

47 Commando
B TROOP

Church

2 Devon
Carrier Platoon
1900 hrs

47 Commando
1400-1600 hrs
D+1 7 June 44

POINT 72

Commander said "Amos, where have you been?" Looking more closely at him and ignoring the ranks of his prisoners, he added, "You haven't had a shave!"'

The Eastern Hill

The German positions on the plateau above Port-en-Bessin to the east were very well developed and dominated the town and the slope up from the port. It was not until several hours after H-Hour that B Troop reached the foot of the Eastern Hill, as they had born the brunt of the fighting in the town. The initial probing attacks up the mined and wired slope were quickly halted by *Spandaus* in concrete *Tobruk* casemates. However, Captain Cousins had identified a possible route up into the enemy position but, as the war diary records, 'Captain Cousins led two attacks up the zig-zag path on eastern feature, which were beaten back'. The attacks came to a halt before dusk, when the enemy mounted a counter-attack, supported by fire from two German flak ships lying alongside the wall of the Port's outer basin. The counter-attack drove the commandos away from the strong point's edge. According to his DSO citation, Major Donnell promptly dealt with the flak ships when 'he went forward and, quickly sizing up the situation, assembled as many of B Troop as he could find. Taking cover in the houses, and with complete disregard for his own safety he personally led the attack on these ships'. The ships duly surrendered.

Meanwhile, 231 Brigade appreciated the difficulties that the Commando was having, with their own ammunition carriers having broken down. Lieutenant Colonel Nevill, with 2 Devon at Longues-sur-

A concrete Tobruk machine gun position on the Eastern Hill overlooking the town and the Western Hill beyond.

A member of a Commando Forward Observation unit takes a bearing on an enemy position. Target information is passed to the ships of the bombarding force.

Mer, records that:

> 'In the meantime news had filtered through that the 47 Marine Commandos were having a very stiff battle at Port-en-Bessin and were being hard-pressed. Our Carrier Platoon therefore went to their immediate assistance and got seriously embroiled on the outskirts of the Port.'

The eight Bren gun carriers were the Battalion's mobile reserve loaded with ammunition. Their light armour and speed gave protection to the crews and enabled the West Countrymen to drive through the three miles of enemy-held territory between the battery and Port-en-Bessin. Sergeant Sear, one of the Carrier Platoon section commanders, was awarded a Military Medal during the infiltration to Port-en-Bessin, when a platoon of *Wehrmacht* infantry attempted to block the route two miles from the port and:

> '... showing a complete disregard for his dangerous situation, with great skill and determination slowly and methodically disengaged his section, inflicting many casualties on the enemy.'

Sergeant Sear covered the move of the remainder of his platoon past the enemy, carefully controlling his men and their fire. The Carrier Platoon 'broke clean' of contact with the enemy and reached Port-en-Bessin in the early evening. The Devons carried additional ammunition in the carriers and used their machine-guns and light mortars to support the commandos, and became heavily embroiled in the fighting on the outskirts of the town.

A Tobruk. One of many concrete machine gun positions above Port-en-Bassin on the Eastern Hill.

Tobruk

The view across Port-en-Bessin from the Western Hill to the Eastern Hill.

Private Jim Wilson identified the platoon's problem:

> 'We came down the hill, past a small Chateau that the Platoon Commander expected to be defended but there were no Germans in sight. My Sarge thought they may be ones that tried to ambush us earlier on. Further down the hill to Bessin, we got more Spandau fire from the high ground into the [open] top of the carrier, which didn't give us much cover. We fired back with Brens but later when we went up the hill we saw that the Spandaus were in concrete Tobruk nests, so we were probably wasting our time.
>
> 'We were under fire on the edge of Bessin all night but we got some Jerries who were trying to get out of the town and up our side of the hill to join the Spandau boys.'

The fighting for the Eastern Hill went on into the night, with the Marines attacking up the slope onto the defended plateau. Commander Edwards wrote:

> 'It was becoming very doubtful if the strong position on the height east of the town could be taken that night, but Captain TF Cousins said that he found and reconnôitred a zig-zag path up the hill and thought that he could get up to the German position with twenty-five men by that route.
>
> 'Captain Cousins was given between forty and fifty men and set out. It was like a miniature replica of the storming of the Heights of Abraham at Quebec by General Wolfe. At dusk Captain Cousins and his men reached the skyline and they at once assaulted the German defences. These they penetrated, while at the same time another troop attacked from the extreme right. This troop also penetrated the German defences, and captured the German commander in his dugout. The German company commander was induced to lead the Marines forward through the mines and summon the remainder of the German Garrison to surrender, and this they did.
>
> 'It was found that the whole top of the hill was honeycombed with dugouts and trenches. Mopping up was therefore a slow business and Captain Cousins unhappily lost his life in the process.'

156

While the fighting was going on in Port-en-Bessin, the group of fifteen Marines of the Main Commando HQ, who had been left to hold Point 72, fell victim to a strong counter-attack from the south-west. Commander Edwards recorded that in the fading light of dusk:

'The Royal Marines unfortunately mistook the Germans at first for Americans, who were expected to arrive at any moment. As a result of this counter-attack, the Germans overran the position on Point 72, capturing the Marines and releasing some of their own prisoners. Most of the Marines subsequently regained the Allied lines.'

D+2 – 2 Devon's Attack on Chateau Fosse Soucy

It was planned that 2 Devon would relieve 47 Commando in Port-en-Bessin as soon as possible, which was not originally expected to be before the morning of D+1. 2 Devon's war diary records:

'8 Jun 44. 0400 hours. Bn received orders to attack westwards to Port-en-Bessin, clearing up enemy strong-points on the coast north of Le Mesnil and Bouffay. Port-en-Bessin was attacked yesterday by 47 RM Commando but they have failed to take it completely though they succeeded in entering the town.'

The entry concludes with the words so often heard in war 'The situation is rather obscure'. Lieutenant Colonel Nevill describes his battalion's advance:

'The post of Le Mesnil surrendered after an artillery and MG [2 Cheshire] bombardment. Two officers and thirty-six other ranks were captured. We suffered no casualties.

'The advance continued rapidly, and it was soon clear that there was no more opposition between us and Port-en-Bessin. We immediately decided to turn south and take over from 47 Commando the high feature known as Pt 72 two miles south of Port-en-Bessin. The hill had been the scene of heavy fighting the day before, and it had changed hands twice.'

With C Company and a squadron of Sherwood Rangers leading, the battalion quickly cleared the Germans from Point 72 and set about digging in, with the tanks deployed in 'hull down' positions on the crest. Meanwhile, the Commanding Officer focused his binoculars on the chateau a thousand yards to the south east that had been pointed out to him as the source of all the trouble on Point 72. The chateau subsequently proved to be the headquarters of the German battalion defending the Port-en-Bessin sector, thought to be 1/726 Infantry Regiment. Lieutenant Colonel Nevill describes the attack:

'C Company relieved the commandos, and preparations were made to attack a large chateau immediately south in full view of the hill. It was known to contain a strong enemy force who were responsible for the trouble with the Marines on the previous day. The top of the hill was subjected to

German defenders lying dead at the entrance to their bunker.

spasmodic fire from the chateau, which made reconnaissance somewhat difficult. A request was made for artillery support [from 8 Armoured Brigade]. *This was only granted after Div HQ were assured that we were in fact going to attack Germans and not Americans; the doubt had arisen as the chateau was actually within American territory. Twice we were asked, and twice we were able to assure them that there could be no mistake. It was at this point that we planned to link up with Lt Col Horner's Combat Team of the American 1st Division; however, they had not yet arrived owing to the very heavy fighting in which they had been involved on the beaches.*

'*The attack on the chateau proved to be a very tricky operation, because the battery in support* [from 147 Field Regiment] *could only be available until 1800 hours. As it was already 1700 hours, there was no time for detailed reconnaissance, and we knew there were two rivers between us and the objective. However, the risk had to be taken, as an attack without artillery fire on the enemy position well dug in amongst the buildings would have been asking for trouble.*

'*The attack started at 1730 hours, with A Company on the right and D Company on the left, supported by a battery of the Essex Yeomanry* [147 Field Regiment] *and a squadron of the Sherwood Rangers, who had their tanks on the very top of the hill. The Cheshire MG platoon was as usual in support, and noble work they did too. All went well until the first river was reached; both companies reported that they were temporarily checked, but a few minutes later, they were across. It was the same story at the second river, only, on this occasion, they were in full view of the enemy, and being subjected to considerable though inaccurate fire. This had taken time; the battery had long since departed for other work; the tanks and machine guns were rapidly running out of ammunition having maintained a very high rate of fire for forty-five minutes. It was a very anxious moment, but owing to the inspiring leadership of both Major Mike Holdsworth and Major Frank Sadler, and to the intrepid gallantry of all ranks under their command, all difficulties were overcome. The final assault* [just before 1930 hours] *was made across the Park to the accompaniment of ringing cheers from all those who were supporting the operation from the top of Hill 72.'*

The medium machine-guns of 2 Cheshire's Number 9 Platoon, mounted in its carriers, had accompanied the Devons westward to Point 72 and fired over 10,000 rounds in support of the attack on Chateau Fosse Soucy. Having born the brunt of the action to clear enemy positions between the Masse de Cradalle and Port-en-Bessin, the attack used up all but a very small amount of the platoon's ammunition. Despite the shortage of ammunition and consequently reduced fire support, 2 Devons Group had maintained pressure on the enemy for long enough for battle to swing in their favour. By 1910 hours, the Battalion watchkeeper was recording in his log 'Chateau captured with approx 40 POW'. Lieutenant Colonel Nevill concluded, with a discrepancy in the number of PWs, that:

'Over a hundred prisoners were captured, and it was discovered that the Chateau was the HQ for that particular area. In praise of our men, a German medical officer said that he had never believed that men could advance across such difficult ground in such perfect order under fire. Although this was but a small operation, it is one of which the Regiment may well be proud.'

The attack was a success but the Commanding Officer was well aware that, if his companies had been halted, they would have been in an unenviable position, pinned down in an open valley. Continuing the attack, despite dwindling ammunition, was the only credible option open to him. Having recognized that a German counter-attack would destroy the companies before they could be resupplied with ammunition, Lieutenant Colonel Nevill ordered the two companies back to stronger, less isolated, positions around Point 72.

Major Mike Holdsworth MC.

'That night the battalion reorganised on Point 72, and had dress circle seats for a good a firework display as anybody could wish to see. The beaches were subjected to bombing all night long; and the flak that was put up by the shore batteries and by the ships had to be seen to be believed.'

At 2130 hours on 8 June, contact was finally made with the 1st US Division

Chateau Fosse Soucy dominated the water meadows and water courses between it and Point 72.

below Point 72 in the village of Escures. The Allies finally had a single linked beachhead.

Port Operations at Bessin

Almost immediately after the strong points on the cliffs had been subdued, Commander Cowley-Thomas RN arrived in the port and set up his Headquarters and began the work of bringing it into use for the landing of stores. Captain Hutchings RN also arrived shortly after the port's capture and was quickly at work on PLUTO (Pipe-Line Under The Ocean). The pipeline was designed to deliver the majority of the vast quantity of fuel needed by a modern army to a spreading network of shore-based pipelines. The first 6-inch TOMBOLA line to deliver fuel from tankers moored at sea came ashore at Port-en-Bessin on D+19 (25 June), and was soon delivering 8,000 tons of fuel per day. It was also found that the port had a greater capacity for landing conventional stores than anticipated. By 14 June the port was handling 1,000 tons of supplies per day. The port and its fuel depot continued to play a significant part in the North West European Campaign long after the battle had moved on to the very borders of Germany

Brigadier Sir Alexander Stanier Bart. being presented with the US Silver Star by General Omar Bradley in recognition of his Brigade's achievements.

CHAPTER TEN

THE MULBERRY HARBOUR

Today, after almost sixty years, the remains of Mulberry Harbour is a unique feature of the coastline west of JIG. Here a broad arc of concrete caissons, designed to last for ninety days, is still visible, even at high tide, nearly sixty years after they were carefully sunk in position. A port had been a planning consideration for both the Allies and the Germans. The second-in-command of the Mulberry project, Vice Admiral Hickling, explained the problem:

'The landing of a huge army with a build-up of millions of tons of equipment and stores called for the appliances of a major port. We might, of course, land over open beaches but that would put the build-up at the mercy of the weather. ... Hitler had said, "If we hold the ports we hold Europe", and the Germans meant to hold the ports: we had a taste of assaulting a major port at Dieppe. To have attacked Cherbourg, for instance, would have been a costly, lengthy and bloody business, forfeiting any element of surprise. Nor was the alternative of landing over open beaches acceptable because no prudent commander was going to leave his build-up to the mercy of the weather in the English Channel.'

The Allied experience at Dieppe caused COSSAC to advocate a landing on a less well defended coastline and that would necessarily be some way away from the heavily defended area surrounding a port. However, there was the problem, correctly identified by Hitler, of building up Allied forces and supplies across beaches more quickly than the Germans could redeploy their reserves. The Allies would have to take their port with them.

As with the specialist armour of 79th Armoured Division, some development work had been undertaken as early as 1941. Work on piers for unloading the ships off a beach had been conducted on behalf of Combined Operations. However, as COSSAC prepared to present its plan to land in Normandy, Churchill gave impetus to the project by issuing to Chief Combined Operations the directive printed overleaf. Shortly afterwards, Major General Sir Harold Wernher was appointed to co-ordinate the fabrication of two ports, each the size of Dover. The essential part of the project was, as described by Churchill, piers that 'float up and down with the tide'. Having seen the memo from the Prime Minister, Sir Bruce White (War Office Assistant Director of Transportation) thought he had the solution:

'I told the Prime Minister that I had frequently been involved in dredging ... I then explained about a dredger which had been seen working

10. Downing Street
Whitehall.

PIERS FOR USE ON BEACHES

C. C. O.
 or deputy.

They must float up and down with the tide. The anchor problem must be mastered. L
me have the best solution worked out. Don't argue the matter. The difficulties will argue for themselves.

30. 5. 42.

in the harbour at Valparaiso during 1924. A storm had broken out and all the ships in the harbour foundered, with the exception of the dredger ... [which] was fitted with three "spuds" or legs. The master of the dredger made use of the vessel's ability to be lifted up and down on the legs by raising her above the waves, thereby avoiding the turbulence.

'Such a technique not only met his [Churchill's] request but also answered the "anchor problem", since the spuds would be firmly placed on the sea bed.'

Thus, the key part of the programme, known as 'SPUD pontoon', was soon on the drawing-board and being built at shipyards in Scotland. In between the SPUDs were concrete pontoons known as 'HIPPO'. The large concrete item lying in the centre of the Arromanches beach at low water is a HIPPO unit. The combination of SPUD and HIPPO would allow ships to come alongside and unload their cargo, and a variant was specially designed to allow speedy unloading of LSTs. Discharging over the beach was slow, as the ship would have to run into the beach and normally have to wait for the tide to rise to get off again. However, the LST SPUD enabled the load of twenty-two tanks and twenty trucks to be driven off in fifteen minutes, vastly speeding the overall LST turnaround time.

WHALE was the code name given to the thousand metres of floating roadway connecting the SPUD pier heads to the land. This roadway was if anything a more challenging scientific problem than the SPUDs. Not only did it have to cope with the tide but survive the rolling sea while bearing

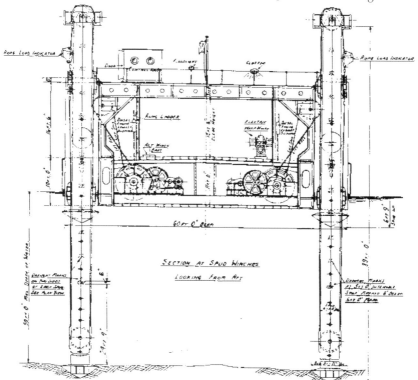

A PHOENIX caisson is moved from its construction site on the south coast of England to one of the concentration areas.

the load of a tank weighing up to forty tons. Numerous ideas were refined down to three trial prototypes. Putting it simply, the eventual design 'comprised a series of linked spans, eighty feet long with a ten foot wide roadway ... weighing twenty-eight tons. ... They allowed free angular movement of one span relative to another of twenty-four degrees and a torsional displacement along the length of each span'. In other words, the flexibility of the roadway gave the structure immense strength. The whole was supported on BEETLE pontoons, which were originally built from steel but, as that material became scarce, all BEETLEs, less those that had a rocky seabed to deal with at low water, were made of concrete. A dozen concrete BEETLEs from the floating roadway still lie on the beach at Arromanches.

Even with their incredible flexibility, the WHALE units would need a harbour wall to protect them. Protection was to be in provided by three elements, GOOSEBERRY, PHOENIX and BOMBARDON. The most conventional means of wave suppression was GOOSEBERRY: the sixty-three old ships that sailed in ballast, arriving off the five invasion beaches on 7 June 1944. Sailing under their own power, they were scuttled a mile off shore to provide an instant breakwater, which reduced the size of waves in order to facilitate landing across the open beaches. In the case of the GOOSEBERRYs on OMAHA and GOLD, they were to be the beginnings of Mulberry A (American) and Mulberry B (British) WHALE units, and PHOENIX caissons followed within days of the landing.

Design, construction and deployment of the PHOENIX caissons was a marvel of wartime achievement, sorely testing Britain's wartime industry, but nothing did more to stretch the Ministry of Supply than PHOENIX. The statistics are awesome; 22,000 men both civilian and military, the latter former construction workers temporarily released from the Services, working for dozens of civilian companies, completed the work. Civil engineer Alan Beckett recalled that:

'In total 147 caissons were constructed in eight wartime months; sixty at the largest size with a displacement of 6,044 tons. When it was all over 330,000 cubic yards of concrete weighing 660,000 tons, 31,000 tons of steel and 1,500,000 super yards of shuttering had been required for their construction.'

Vice Admiral Hickling described the end product and production:

'There were half a dozen different sizes of Phoenix depending on the depth of water in which they were to be planted, for they formed not only the outer breakwater but also the side arms. The A1 – the biggest, was 200ft long, by 60ft high and 40ft beam. These 'blocks of flats' had to satisfy various conditions, the first of which was that they had to be towable, and that is why they were given swim (upswept) ends...

The question was where to build these things... We tried to get dry docks but the majority of these were already in use on shipping repair and a lot of jobs in connection with the assault itself... However, big holes were

SPUD piers with the 'up' and 'down' route WHALE piers.

scratched on the banks of tidal waters such as the Thames and Southampton Water, and the first 14ft of the Phoenixes were built there; when this was done, the bank was broken down to let the water in and the sections were floated out and taken to adjacent wharves where they were completed. ... The first unit took about four months to build, but as things went on this was reduced to two months.'

BOMBARDONs were the most controversial part of the Mulberry project. Produced and deployed by the Navy rather than the Army, this seaward element was designed to reduce the buffeting that GOOSEBERRY and PHOENIX would receive from the waves. Vice-Admiral Hickling again provides an insight:

'Outside each harbour, it was decided to put down a mile of floating breakwater called the 'Bombardon'. This was an entirely novel form of breakwater ... Lochner, Lieutenant RNVR, was sitting one summer's afternoon alongside a swimming pool where a lilo was floating. He noticed wavelets breaking on the windward side, while on the lee it was calm.'

The eventual design was a string of two-hundred-foot-long units, with a Maltese cross-like profile twenty-five feet in depth and beam. Securely

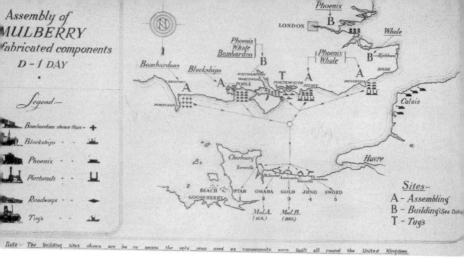

Assembly of
MULBERRY
fabricated components
D - 1 DAY

Legend —

Bombardons shown thus -
Blockships
Phoenix
Pierheads
Roadways
Tugs

Sites:-
A - Assembling
B - Building (See Note)
T - Tugs

Note :- The building sites shown are by no means the only ones used as components were built all round the United Kingdom.

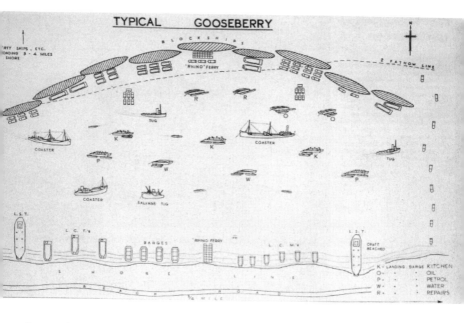

TYPICAL   GOOSEBERRY

K - LANDING BARGE KITCHEN
O - " " OIL
P - " " PETROL
W - " " WATER
R - " " REPAIRS

anchoring the units in deep water was a problem that some had little faith could be solved, but, in their first week, they were able to suppress waves by forty per cent, allowing Liberty ships to unload outside of the main breakwater. However, the BOMBARDONs did not last long, as, designed to cope with Force 6 - 7 wind and waves, they eventually broke loose after thirty hours of the storm (Force 7 - 9) that broke on D+13 (19 June).

Ammunition Pier

LST Pier

Small Boat Shelter

MULBERRY B at Arromanches. This photograph was taken on a busy day in August 1944.

Deployment

The various components were kept as widely spread as possible until the last moment and, also in the interest of security, there was to be no rehearsal. Elements of the ports were gathered in the Solent between Lymington in the west and Selsey Bill to the east. The Germans could not have failed to notice strange items being towed through the Straights of Dover from the Thames Estuary but they never guessed their true purpose. Indeed those Mulberry units, deliberately left at Dungeness, reinforced the enemy view that the *Pas de Calais* was the Invasion's objective, even though they were not sure what they were for. Admiral Hickling recalled the mixed feelings about Mulberry being incorporated into the FORTITUDE

deception plans:

> 'In order to soothe the soldiers – who were naturally rather anxious about their Whales and Phoenix – we got a professor to work out the probability of these units at Dungeness being damaged by the enemy's long range guns. He reckoned that if the enemy fired 1,000 rounds – all he could in the time – there would only be eleven hits. So the Army was placated. In point of fact, they were not fired on at all. The enemy went on firing at Dover, so everyone was happy – except possibly Dover'.

Many men, ranging from Royal Artillery gun crews, through field engineers to ordinary seamen from the Royal Navy and Merchant Marine were drafted into the Mulberry project at the last moment. So tight was security that the first many of them knew of the part they, and the piece of strange equipment under their charge was to play, was when they were finally isolated from the shore.

Admiral Hickling was responsible for getting the harbours across the Channel with a fleet of one hundred and thirty two tugs:

'The first Mulberry left harbour in the evening of D-Day. For the purposes of planning, we had worked out an integrated towing programme, because each unit had to be moved into the harbour in its proper place and proper order at the proper time. Of course, we realized that with so many unknown factors, including enemy action, our programme could never be strictly adhered to, but it provided a very good guide. In our planning we had allowed for a towing speed of three knots – actually an average speed of four knots was achieved ... We allowed for a 20 per cent loss of the units to be towed – our losses of Bombardons, Phoenixes and Pierheads were negligible; our losses of pier roadways due to bad weather was of the order of 50 per cent.

'Each night, depending on the weather forecast, the following units were dispatched to each Mulberry: 4 to 5 Phoenixes, 6 Bombardons, 2 or 3 Pierheads, 4 or 5 sections of pier roadways.'

Arriving ahead of the first Mulberry units was Brigadier Walter, who recalled the arrival of Headquarters Port Construction Force (PCF) aboard a former Clyde paddle steamer HMS *Aristocrat*:

'We arrived at our station off shore at Arromanches before dawn on D+1. At first light, to our consternation, we saw German soldiery through glasses on the high ground to the west of the town. This meant that right at the start our plans were adrift because it had been planned that Arromanches should be liberated by units of 231 Brigade on D-Day so that the PCF units could begin to move in on D+1 and start on the very tight schedule of planting the harbour...

'By about 0900 hrs the Germans seemed to disappear and an American DUKW with two dead Americans aboard drifted through the Piccadilly Circus of shipping into HMS Aristocrat and the sailors made it fast – here was the unplanned but perfect way to get ashore. My driver, Corporal Antony, claimed to know how to drive a DUKW and so we set off and arrived at Gold Item beach between Cabane and Asnelles.'

At 13.50 hours on D+1, Brigadier Walter watched the Navy scuttle the first CORNCOB (HMS *Alynbank*) in the chain of ships that were to make up the GOOSEBERRY breakwater. According to Brigadier Walter:

'Everything went wrong – she settled too slowly and the tugs failed to hold her in line as she sank and she ended up more or less at right angles to the intended line of the breakwater. This was a bad start but the Navy immediately learned the lesson and in the following days successfully planted their part of the breakwater.'

Many sailors working on the construction of the harbour, preferring to

Block ships or CORNCOBs being sunk in position to form instant GOOSEBERRY shelters.

occupy less cramped berths, took up residence in the CORNCOBs' compartments still above the waterline. Eventually they became a warren of offices, stores, workshops and accommodation for the crews of the one hundred DUKWs and one hundred and fifty ferries and lighters at work in the harbour.

Following behind the CORNCOBs were the PHOENIX caissons. As mentioned above most crossings, though nerve wracking for their largely powerless crews, were successful However, Robert Pintar's crossing on the night of D+1 / D+2 was far from uneventful:

'We were to be the second caisson to arrive just before dawn. It was dark: the skies were full of planes, ships all around, red skies on the coast of France, sounds of war gave chills up the spine. Standing on the stern deck watching the tug towing us at 01.15 hours, I heard a splash – splash and a hissing sound on the port side and saw two torpedoes skimming along the surface that crossed our bows and aft of the tug – missed us! ... I was speechless, then shouted to the crew below, "Torpedoes, torpedoes", ... At

this point we could hear the deep-throated diesel sound of the enemy E-Boat and two more torpedoes splashing as they were launched. We watched them hissing along in a foam of death towards us. One along the port side and the other along the starboard side, both from the stern – missed again. We were all on deck now looking and listening. ... Off in the distance – dead centre of our stern, we heard the "splash splash"; one torpedo to the starboard. Harry and I leaned over the rail to watch. The torpedo slammed into our stern with an almighty KA-BOOM. We were thrown twenty feet into the air and by the time we landed the caisson was listing thirty degrees and sinking fast. We slid and tumbled down the deck into the cold sea. The sinking caisson sucked us down with it to the bottom of the Channel, about twenty-five fathoms deep, ten miles off France. ... When we came up to the surface I found the life raft.'

However, the first PHOENIX were settled along the five fathom line on 10 June and the harbour began to take shape, with the first loads coming ashore via WHALE units on 14 June (D+8). Within days, the totals handled in the port grew to almost 5,000 tons and 1,400 vehicles per day. This, combined with unloading over the beaches and behind the GOOSEBERRYs on the other beaches, not only maintained those formations already ashore and in action, but ensured that the Allies matched the German rates of build-up in Normandy.

Belatedly the Germans seemed to realize the significance of the harbours and began nightly air raids. Alan Polglaze, Captain of HMS *Aristocrat* recalled:

'At night German planes frequently came over but much to our regret we were not allowed to open fire, since this could betray our position and harbour activity. Of course, one night the inevitable happened, a gun opened fire and the next thing we were all at it! The bells started to ring and we were ordered to cease-fire immediately.'

Threats of dire consequences were made against any one who infringed these orders. Although, as German attacks increased and Allied air-space control over the harbour improved, there was a nightly firework display of anti-aircraft tracer, there were very few enemy aircraft casualties.

The Storm

Much has been written about the effects of the storm in relation to tonnage landed and the overall effect of the Mulberry harbours. However, even a superficial analysis points to the fact that worthwhile comparisons are impossible, as the British and Americans collected data on a totally different basis. Captain Alan Harris of 933 Port Construction and Repair Company RE recounts the basic facts about the storm:

'A gale blew from the morning of D+13 (19 June) until the night of D+19 (22 June), Direction north north-east, Force 6-7 most of the time

This aerial photograph clearly shows the effectiveness of the blocks and caissons. Rough sea can be seen at the bottom of this picture perfectly calm water where ships are unloading men and stores. three long pontoon causeways stretch to the beaches.

Ammunition
Pier

Dry
Dock
Ships

HMS
Alynbank

[gusting Force 9]; *waves were a mean height of 8-9ft with a maximum of 12 – 14 ft. The depression was not intense nor were the winds tempestuous, but they blew from the same quarter for four days and, with a fetch of 100 miles, stirred up a dangerous sea.'*

The point to note is that it was not the wind but the waves that did so much damage, destroying the American Mulberry of Omaha and damaging Mulberry B.

What had gone wrong? Firstly, as recounted by Captain Harris, 'The meteorological warning was short: the depression came up from Eastern Europe, not from, as is usual, the Atlantic: the Met people, without weather stations to the east, were blind in that quarter'. Secondly, as recorded by Brigadier Walter:

'Mulberry A failed for the following reasons: owing to a decision to enlarge their harbour, the Americans sank their Phoenix units in deeper water, which reduced their freeboard and led to their collapse. They failed to deploy the full complement of anchors to secure the roadway and loose craft including Bombardons did considerable damage.'

Thirdly, as noted by several authorities, work in constructing Mulberry A had been carried out far more quickly than that on Mulberry B. CORNCOBs were sunk leaving gaps in the GOOSEBERRY wall of blockships, whereas the British carefully overlapped their CORNCOBs to present a near-solid wall. However, it would be invidious to lay all the blame at the door of the American Navy Engineers, as they also had little training and, in addition, did not have the experience that the British had gained during Mulberry's development and trials.

The storm led to some dramatic moments in Mulberry B. Captain Alan Harris's record again explains how following the belated Met warning:

'Action was immediate. Lt Col Maris ordered all floating roadway moorings to be checked, harbour tugs to be fuelled and victualled fully and to ready to grapple and tow away craft out of control; parties of Sappers to be allocated to various emergency tasks, orders given to fire on any craft attempting to come alongside pierheads, pontoons, etc, all craft to windward of the pierheads and piers to up-anchor and move to leeward. Warning shots were fired by the Bofors cannon on the Phoenix (reputed to be more dangerous than the Luftwaffe, they had already punched holes in the funnel of HMS Rodney); Capt Witcomb, officer in charge of pierheads, was told to hoist the pierheads up the spuds as far as he dared.

'Mulberry was intended to provide shelter for 1,000 small craft in case of storm. In the event, many times that many came in for shelter from the beaches to the east. ... To be awakened by some soldier with orders to sling the hook and move somewhere else (orders supported by dire threats) was not welcomed by Navy skippers, who after a rough night at sea, had finally found shelter.

Heavy seas smash up the causeway to the beach.

'Most damage was done by loose craft hitting the LST and floating pierheads and the easterly spud pontoons. An LST, crewless, doors swinging, struck a stores pierhead and was smashing both itself and the pierhead to pieces, when out of the murk came the tugs, some British, some American, who grappled and towed it away.'

The protective patrols in the harbour, mentioned above, were vital to preventing the build-up of powerless craft that carried away the Americans' floating roadway. It is alleged that, during the storm, 'Brigadier Walter drew his pistol to induce a crew to sink their powerless craft'.

The part played by the BOMBARDONs in the storm is controversial and laced with inter-Service rivalry. What is not disputed is that they held for the first thirty hours of the storm and no doubt contributed to the reduction of wave effect during the early part of the storm. However, the BOMBARDONs were deployed in only one line, not two (as ordered by Admiral Ramsey on D/D+1), and were anchored in water twice as deep as intended. Consequently, they failed, and the two-hundred-foot-long steel structures were driven towards the PHOENIX caissons where the Army allege that they did considerable damage and contributed to the destruction of units in the central breakwater. The Navy deny this but what is not in doubt is that one BOMBARDON was blown into the harbour and caused considerable damage before it was engaged with a hand held anti-tank weapon, holed and sunk. The amount of vital sheet steel directed into the construction of the BOMBARDONs and their relative lack of effect have been consistent sources of debate over the years.

In the aftermath of the storm, General Eisenhower confirmed that

Mulberry A was to be abandoned, leaving only the GOOSEBERRY and remains of the PHOENIX units to protect a much slower process of landing over the beach. This greatly increased the turn-around times of LSTs, etc. However, the American Engineers salvaged and repaired units of various types to make good losses in Mulberry B, and within two days tonnages landed were almost normal. By D+23 record tonnages of vehicles, ammunition and stores were flowing ashore to support Montgomery's Operation EPSOM.

While never handling anything near the majority of Allied men, equipment and stores coming into Normandy, Mulberry was an essential insurance policy. As far as the Navies were concerned, Mulberry was a force multiplier for the landing craft fleet, thus building into Allied plans a margin of error against the one unpredictable force Hitler had in his favour – the weather in the English Channel.

Epilogue

In the late autumn of 1944, the Mulberry Harbour's work was completed – once the island of Walcheren on the mouth of the Scheldt had been captured and the port of Antwerp opened. Parts of the harbour were then reused or recycled. Some PHOENIX caissons were pumped out and refloated to be used to help repair the breach in the Walcheren dyke. Parts of the WHALE roadway were taken inland and used as semi-permanent replacements for the Bailey bridges, which were needed for the advance into Germany. After the war, with steel at a premium in war-damaged Europe, scrap dealers scavenged anything metal that was removable. For example one CORNCOB was refloated and taken back to Scotland to be broken up. Today, all that remains visible are the concrete caissons, twelve BEETLEs and a HIPPO pontoon – remnants of a technological idea that allowed the Allies to achieve operational surprise through lateral thinking.

CHAPTER ELEVEN

231 BRIGADE D-DAY TOUR

The tour described here will enable the visitor to travel around the scene of 231 Brigade Group's battles fought in the coastal areas west of GOLD Beach. It is assumed that the visitor will have transport, be it minibus, car or bicycle. However, the area between JIG / le Hamel and Arromanches is short enough for a six-mile round trip walk which takes in most of the key sites. With or without transport, to reach the scene of the fighting at Points 54 and 72, it will be necessary for the visitor to take short walks.

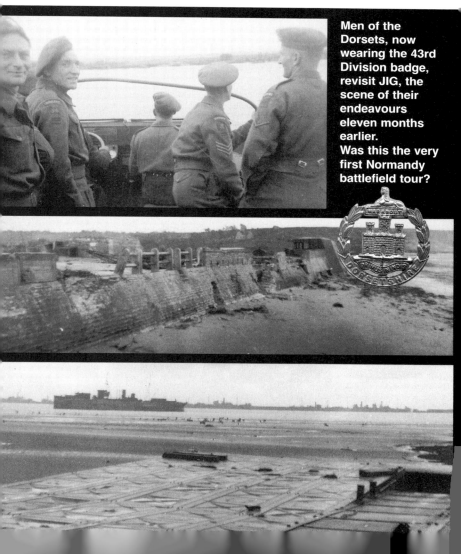

Men of the Dorsets, now wearing the 43rd Division badge, revisit JIG, the scene of their endeavours eleven months earlier.
Was this the very first Normandy battlefield tour?

The tour starts at Wiederstandnest 36 on JIG Beach to the east of le Hamel. Arromanches is nearest town and is signposted from Ouisterham, the Caen Peripherique, the **N13** and from Bayeux. From **Arromanches take the D 514** and turn off this road towards the sea, just to the east of Asnelles / le Hamel. At the time of writing, the road to the coast has signposts advertising oystermen's stores (Location d'Huitres). Cars should use the parking places and minibuses should park so as not to block the ramp down to the beach, which oystermen use at low water and other boatowners at high water.

Jig Beach ❶

How much of the beach can be seen is dependent on the state of the tide. At high water, the sea leaves only a narrow strip of beach before the sand dunes to the east of the car park. At low mean low water, the tide on the gently sloping beach goes out far enough for the visitor to walk to the nearest piece of Mulberry Harbour. After storms it is occasionally possible to see the muddy peat outcrops on the beach that

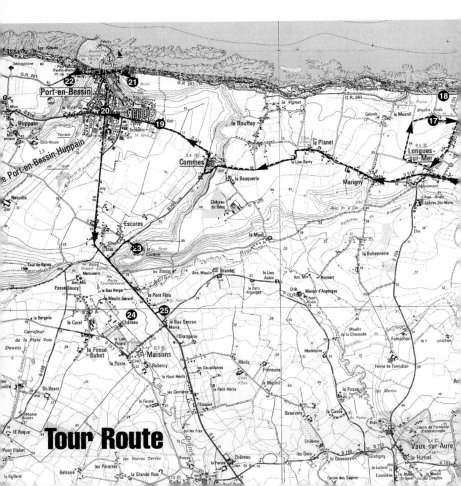

Tour Route

The 20mm casemate for anti-aircraft/anti-boat gun at WN36, as it was in 1944 and present-day condition after sixty years of coastal erosion. Behind it on the beach are a number of troop shelters.

so concerned the Combined Operations planners and necessitated the development of crossing devices such as the Bobbin.

The assault engineers and 'Funnies' of 79th Armoured Division touched down at just over half tide, with the sea level rising, with the beach obstacles still visible at H-Hour. However, fire from unsuppressed defences in le Hamel prevented the Royal Engineers from clearing the obstacles and, consequently, subsequent flights of landing craft had to run the gauntlet of mine-tipped obstacles.

1 Hampshire landed to the left and right of this point, with their intended beach being further west near le Hamel. A pair of binoculars will help visitors identify the casemate, immediately inland of the white tower at le Hamel that contained the 77mm gun that caused so many problems on this stretch of beach.

Widerstandneste 36 ❷

Coastal erosion has left most of WN36's concrete positions lying partly buried on the beach. Most obvious is the octagonal casemate that contained a dual-purpose 20mm anti-boat/anti-aircraft gun. It is possible to identify where other positions lay using the maps and air photographs on page 62 of this book, as far back as the line of the old coast road. A part of WN36 extended to the west of the beach ramp and now lies under the modern houses opposite the car park.

Number Six Gap ❸

A three-quarter mile walk along the beach and dunes will take the visitor past the area where 1 Dorset's companies landed, to the Number 6 Gap where most of the Sherwood Rangers' Shermans and the self-propelled guns landed. Visitors electing to take this walk in summer months should be aware that they could come across the odd nudist in the sand dunes. Landing at The Point, Number 6 Breaching Team consisted of three AVREs mounting 'Pusher', 'Bobbin' and 'Fascine', two Sherman Crabs (flails), a D7 armoured Bulldozer and a detachment from 73 Field Squadron RE. They created a short gap through the minefield to the Lateral or Old Coast Road, which at this point comes very close to the beach. Walk back along the Old Coast Road, noting the obstacle that the marsh would have been to movement inland. The site of the large crater that caused the delays to the armour getting inland can not be definitely identified, as the road was repaired after the war. Cut back across the dunes to the car park via one of the tracks before reaching the end gate.

les Roquettes ❹

It was through this point that most of 231 Brigade Group made their way inland. Air recce had identified enemy activity in buildings in the area of the oyster sheds. Brigadier Stanier formed his first

Number Six Gap

Old Coast Road

Photograph taken late morning D-Day – Number Six Gap

headquarters here and held in this area, as Brigade Reserve, B Company 1 Dorset, who had made their slow and muddy way across the marsh from the area of Number 6 Gap. Also in this area, 2 Cheshire's machine guns were positioned in case 69 Brigade had not cleared the enemy from the Mont Fleury – Meuvaines Ridge. By early afternoon, the SP guns of 90 and 147 Field Regiments were deploying into their first gun positions in the fields to the south.

It should be noted that in 1944 construction of the D 514 had been abandoned and was marked as such on the maps.

231 Brigade Memorial ❺

Drive into Asnelles/le Hamel. **Park at the crossroads** (Place Alexander Stanier) near the memorials. The largest memorial was raised by the French inhabitants in memory of 231 Brigade shortly after the war. During the fiftieth Anniversary commemorations, a black marble memorial to 2 South Wales Borderer was unveiled. This battalion, after a delay during which the assault battalions moved inland, landed with 56 Brigade on JIG Green and passed through 2 Devons at Ryes and advanced to Bayeux.

This is the area from which 1 Hampshires attacked into le Hamel from Asnelles, and in the buildings on the southern side of the square Major David Warren controlled the battle from his Tac HQ.

le Hamel East ❻

From Place Alexander Stanier take **Rue The Devonshire Regiment** and **turn left at the crossroads**. Park in the car park avoiding obscuring the view from the casemate eastwards.

77mm
casemate

Tobruk
MG position

Chateau Asnelles

In the car park can be seen a Tobruk machine gun position and the casemate that contained the captured Polish 77mm gun, which dominated this area of the coast. Looking east along JIG Beach, it can be readily appreciated how this gun enfiladed 231 Brigade and how it drove the landings of armour further east to the Point. The casemate was attacked frontally by an SP artillery piece of 147 Field Regiment and an AVRE from the rear during the final phase of 1 Hampshire's clearance of le Hamel. The gun was originally thought to be an 88mm and is incorrectly recorded as such in war diaries, some unit histories and on the memorial plaques. However, Combined Ops experts completing a report on the defences, positively identified it as a Polish 77mm.

Inland from the casemate, the Sanatorium has been demolished and replaced by housing. Beyond the houses, Chateau Asnelles survives and can be identified from the oblique air photograph on pages 68 and 82.

le Hamel West ❼

Leaving the 77mm casemate, and driving west along the front, the sea wall built by the Germans, complete with Tobruk positions, can be seen. It is not possible to drive all the way along the front to le Hamel West. Park where possible before the road turns inland. Many of the houses were defended and have either been repaired, replaced or demolished. However, it is possible to identify some buildings from the photograph taken from low flying aircraft before D-Day. This area was cleared by C/A Company 1 Hampshire with the support of AVREs who belatedly arrived to support them.

50 mm Anti-Tank Gun Casemate ❽

Follow the road inland through the houses and turn right on the **D 514** towards **Arromanches**. At the end of the village, **park by a small restaurant** near a Parc Huitres. Waking down to the 50mm gun casemate on the sea wall, look for the associated, overgrown, concrete shelters in the gardens to the right. This was the final part of le Hamel to be cleared, but, being attacked from the landward side, the open 50mm gun casemate afforded little cover to its gunners.

This ramp was the site of the exit from the Mulberry Harbour's Rhino Ferry Wharf. Several hundred yards further west, at the foot of the Cabane cliffs, was where the LST pier came ashore.

Ryes ❾

Return to your car and take the **D 205** towards **le Carrefour** and **Ryes**. To your left is the broad open valley of la Grande Riviere, along which 2 Devon advanced to Ryes. To the right is the ridge of high ground that extends from Cabane to Ryes, which is crowned by Point 54 (we will return to this high ground later in the tour). Much of the close country that surrounded Ryes, and provided cover to the Germans who had been rushed to block the British advance inland, has gone. Some hedgerows and orchards still exist and give an impression of the difficulties that the Devons would have faced. They eventually outflanked the Germans by following the road into the village.

On the evening of 6 June, 56 Brigade passed through 2 Devon and advanced to Bayeux, which they occupied the following morning without a serious fight.

CWGC Cemetery Ryes ❿

Although not strictly in the area covered by this

Battleground volume, the Ryes CWGC Cemetery is well worth a visit. Follow the Green and white CWGC signs from the centre of Ryes to the cemetery, which is **a mile to the east**.

The cemetery is the last resting-place of 979 Allied and German soldiers, sailors and airmen. In a remote location, it is the most beautiful of the Allied cemeteries in Normandy, even though it lacks the scale of Bayeux or St Laurent. A visit here is always an emotional experience. The grave register and visitors' books are located in the pavilion to the right of the Great Cross. Two plots of German graves are to be found at the left and right rear of the cemetery.

Most of the graves do not date from D Day, as bodies in the immediate area of the beach were in most cases returned to the UK. However, some 231 Brigade casualties can be found here.

Point 54 ⓫ – Walking Route

Return through **Ryes** to the **D 205**. Turn left in **la Carrefour** and park near the farm avoiding blocking farm entrances and tracks. Walk back to the crossroads and turn right back towards Ryes. After 200 yards **take a right turn off the road** at the outskirts of Buhot. This track and paths on the hill are public rights of way. The leading company of 1 Dorset attempted to cross the field on the right but was forced to fight its way up the hillside via the path. In the copse at the top of the path are remnants of the Point 54 field fortifications that had been dug in the weeks immediately before D-Day and were an unwelcome surprise to the Dorsets.

In the valley west of Point 54, is the wood that was cleared by D Company 1 Dorset during the Battalion's initial approach to the Puits d'Herode strong point. Puits d'Herode lay immediately to the north of the wood. The tanks of the Sherwood Rangers who joined the battle, climbed the ridge further to the south. Turn right and head down hill. Before reaching the farm at the bottom of the hill, turn left up a track that runs between the wood and Puits d'Herode. The Wood is private property and, other than in very dry years, all that can be seen of the Puits d'Herode infantry position is the concrete base of the French-style ablution block! It is easy to appreciate why the German 352nd Division took up defensive positions on this ridge, as it gave the Atlantic Wall some additional depth behind Arromanches. Walk back down past the farm to your car.

Puits d'Herode and view of Point 54 ⓫ᵃ – Non-Walking Tour

From the le Carrefour crossroads, drive **five hundred yards** up the hill and park your car. You are now in the centre of the Puits d'Herode infantry strong-point. Point 54 and the wood can be identified from the map on page 94.

The 'Half Troop Position' – Cabane ⑫

Return to the le Carrefour crossroads, **turn left** on the **D 205** back towards le Hamel. At the junction with the **D 514** near the Parc Huitres turn left towards **Cabane** and **Arromanches**. This road, that runs past the church and through the centre of the battery, did not exist in 1944. Just after the church, in the road cutting, look out for a casemate on top of the slope to the left and park. On the inland side of the road is one of the gun casemates and a large HQ / shelter bunker, while on the seaward side amongst the estate of holiday homes is a further casemate and other shelters including Tobruk positions. Most of these are incorporated into dwellings or their gardens.

The Radar Station and Arromanches East ⑬ ⑭

The area on the cliff east of Arromanches is dominated by a viewing point and a frequently busy car park. The concrete constructions are now perilously close to the cliff-top thanks to nearly sixty years of erosion. The obvious concrete block with sloping sides was the base of the Giant Wurtzburg radar. Some of the power and control bunkers are accessible. Walking towards Arromanches, a viewing platform is passed and, before reaching the 360 Cinema, there is a memorial to the Royal Engineers. The 360 Cinema, mainly using American footage, portrays activities in the Arromanches area but is worth a visit, especially if the weather is inclement.

Little remains of the upper Arromanches East defences, as these were mainly field positions, but the arc of fire that these positions would have had can be readily appreciated.

Arromanches ⑮

In low season, **drive down to the square** on the seafront at Arromanches (pay and display). However, in high season, it is often worth leaving the car in the Radar Station car park and walking down the steep track (less than five minutes) into Arromanches centre. On the way down, an 77mm casemate is passed on the left, surmounted by a Sherman painted in the colours of the Free French. Following the destruction of Mulberry A in 'The Storm', a part of the French Leclerc Division landed through Mulberry B at Arromanches.

The main feature of the square, very much geared to tourism, is the D-Day Landings Museum. This building, surrounded by vehicles and weapons, concentrates on the Mulberry, although it also covers the landings and Normandy Campaign in general, through video and audio/visual displays. The Museum is well worth a visit – groups should book. A memorial to Brigadier Stanier can be found alongside the sea wall near the museum.

There are plenty of restaurants, hotels and a perfectly acceptable municipal campsite in Arromanches. The town is an excellent base for exploring the D-Day cost, not only for its central position but for the amenities it offers the visitor.

Arromanches West ⑯

This area can be reached by a short walk along the seafront past the two westerly beach access ramps (to the general stores pier and the ammunition pier respectively) or, alternatively, by car en route to the next stand. At the time of writing coastal erosion is eating into the road, so beware.

Longues-sur-Mer Battery ⑰ ⑱

Follow the road signs out of Arromanches towards Port-en-Bessin on the **D65/D514**. From the turning to Tracy and Manvieux (both 1 Hampshire D-Day patrol objectives), signs to the battery can be followed. In the village of Longues-sur-Mer, **turn right** at the traffic lights and head north, towards the coast on the D104. The four Kriegsmarine built casemates ⑰ are a short walk from the car park and are the only major battery to still mount its guns, post-war scrap metal merchants having been kept at bay. The Number 4 casemate and its gun owes its current state not to Allied action, but to an unfortunate accident in the days after D-Day, when a visitor managed to ignite the ammunition propellant in the casemate. The observation bunker ⑱ is down the track to the cliffs from between guns 2 and 3. Climbing up to the upper observation platform is relatively easy, but a visitor hoping to explore the battery command post/radio room and machine-gun positions will need wellington boots and a good torch. The casemate contains several inches of mud and water and the greatest care should be taken if entering.

Port-en-Bessin (19) (20) (21)  ⓳ ⓴ ㉑

Follow the one-way circuit from the Battery's car park, back towards the D514. **Turn right** at the traffic lights towards Port-en-Bessin. Keep an eye out for the new 47 Commando memorial ⓳ (unveiled in 1997) on the right-hand side of the road. Continue on past the civil cemetery and turn right at the major cross-roads towards the centre of town. The church ⓴ used by the Commandos as a rendezvous and firm base is a hundred yards further on. Parking can be difficult in Port-en-Bessin, which is busy most of the time. Park when the opportunity presents itself alongside the fishing boats in the inner basin or in the area surrounding the outer basin. Both parking areas are a short walk across the lock gate to the foot of the Port-en-Bessin East defences. Covering the small piece of beach to the east of the harbour is a casemate with a memorial plaque to 47 Commando mounted on it. Take the path up the slope past the seventeenth century tower. Reaching the plateau and the Port-en-Bessin East defences ㉑ it is easy to follow the overgrown trench lines from position to position. This is one of the most extensive and best preserved Wiederstandneste on the Invasion Coast and is well worth taking a good look around. The difficult task facing the commandos is self-evident.

The original 47 Commando memorial on a casemate at the foot of the Eastern Hill.

Port-en-Bessin West ㉒

The Port-en-Bessin West defences can be clearly seen from the edge of the plateau on which the Eastern defences were built. Those who wish to inspect the western defences more closely should be aware that most of the casemates have been incorporated in the post-war development in this area.

Point 72 (Pt 69 Mont Cavalier) ㉓

Point 72 (marked as Point 69 on modern maps) is also on private land. However, driving south from Port-en-Bessin and turning left on to the D100 to Escures takes the visitor to the northern edge of the feature. From here it is possible to appreciate the significance of the position to 47 Commando, 2 Devon and 352nd Division.

The Chateau ㉔

The attack on the Chateau can be best appreciated by returning to the **D6** and turning left towards Bayeux. Park after half a mile and the Chateau can be seen across the valley that 2 Devon had to cross with rapidly diminishing fire support.

To return to **Bayeux**, continue to follow the **D6** south and to **Arromanches,** turn back north towards Port-en-Bessin and follow the signs on the **D514** east. **OMAHA Beach** and the American Sector is best reached by following the D514 west from Port-en-Bessin. The US Cemetery is signed from the town.

The D-Day Wrecks Museum ㉕

This museum on the D6 south of Port-en-Bessin is worth a visit.

ORDER OF BATTLE
231 INFANTRY BRIGADE GROUP
(Assault Phase)

231 INFANTRY BRIGADE

231st Infantry Brigade Headquarters-Command

231st Infantry Brigade Signal Squadron-Communication

2nd Battalion, The Devonshire Regiment-Brigade Reserve battalion

1st Battalion, The Dorsetshire Regiment-Left Assault battalion

1st Battalion, The Hampshire Regiment-Right Assault battalion

90th Field Regiment RA (25-pounder SP (Ram)-Fire support from LCT

288th (or 'C') Battery, 102 (Northumberland Hussars Yeomanry) Anti-Tank Regiment RA (2 troops of 3-inch M10 Tank Destroyer & 2 troops of 6-pounders)

295th Field Company RE (one platoon allocated to each infantry battalion)-General support

C Company 2nd Battalion, The Cheshire Regiment (Machine Gun)

14 Platoon, 2nd Battalion, The Cheshire Regiment (Heavy Mortar)

DETACHMENTS FROM 8 ARMOURED BRIGADE

Nottinghamshire (Sherwood Rangers) Yeomanry (2 Squadrons DD and 2 Squadrons normal Shermans)

147th (Essex Yeomanry) Field Regiment RA (25-pounder SP) Ram-Fire support from LCT

DETACHMENTS FROM 79th ARMOURED DIVISION

B Squadron Westminster Dragoons (Flails)

Troop C Squadron 141st Regiment RAC (Crocodiles)

82nd Squadron, 6th Assault Royal Engineers (Churchill AVRE)-Armoured Beach Assault

235th Field Park Company RE (Armoured Bulldozers)-Improvement of beach exits

50TH NORTHUMBRIAN DIVISIONAL TROOPS

73rd Field Company RE-Clearance of underwater obstacles

Detachments 200th Field Ambulance RAMC

HQ and Platoon, 243rd Provo Company RCMP

COMBINED OPERATIONS TROOPS

7th RM Signals Unit

21st Beach Signal Section

Q Commando Royal Navy

1st Royal Marines Armoured Support Regiment (Centaur and Porpoise)

47th Commando Royal Marines (under command for landing)

B Troop, Number 1 Bombardment Unit (Forward Observer Bombardment teams)

55th Balloon Unit RAF

INDEX